EVERYDAY
NAKED

*Sacred & Profane
Morsels of Truth*

Mary Bartnikowski

CELESTIALARTS
Berkeley, California

This book is dedicated to
Sukie Mergener, Wolfe Price
and
Michael Price

CELESTIALARTS

P.O. Box 7123
Berkeley, California 94707
e-mail:order@tenspeed.com
website:www@tenspeed.com

Distributed in Canada by Ten Speed Canada, in the United Kingdom and Europe by Airlift Books, in New Zealand by Tandem Press, in Australia by Simon & Schuster Australia, in Singapore and Malaysia by Berkeley Books, and in South Africa by Real Books.

Cover and interior design by Greene Design
Cover photograph by Mary's darling husband
Interior illustrations by our favorite gal, Mary Bartnikowski

Library of Congress Cataloging-in-Publication Data

Bartnikowski, Mary.
    Everyday naked : sacred & profane morsels of truth / Mary
Bartnikowski.
       p. cm.
      ISBN 0-89087-876-5 (pbk.)
      I. Title.
    PN6162.B299 1998
    814'.54--dc21   98-18810
                                                       CIP

First printing, 1998
Printed in the United States

1 2 3 4 5 6 7—02 01 00 99 98

Acknowledgements

For Sukie, who said, "Are you writing?" every time I spoke with her and asked me to dedicate my book to her. She said, "Even if I'm gone I'll know." She believed in me when lots of people thought I should just shut up.

For Wolfe, who told me, "Why don't you stop writing and work on publishing the book?" You have taught me far more than I have taught you.

For Michael, my loverman, who is telling total strangers, "Don't wear clothes when you read this book because you'll pee in your pants laughing." And for being the most flame-roasted person in this book. I am eternally incredulous that you can laugh at yourself. I love you. Let's stay married forever.

For Veronica Randall, my publisher / mentoring goddess, who plucked me out of obscurity and opened her arms wide saying, "Welcome to the world of Publishing!" Your trainloads of enthusiasm and energy have sent me soaring and railroaded this book into being.

For my father, who is the wittiest guy I know and also the cutest. Let's go on more dates, Dad! I liked seeing you do somersaults over my book. You, who gave me a loud and sonorous laugh by virtue of your DNA and called only me "Princess" and taught me how to laugh at myself.

For Brenda, who makes my face hurt from laughing and keeps me floating above ground with her wisdom, wit, Frederick's of Hollywood gifts and her movie star looks in Marilyn Monroe pajamas. We're two peas in a king bed. We'll always have Maui and each other and the Sky Booth.

For Angie, whom I love dearly. You are the rockin'est babe on the planet. You shine so brilliantly it knocks my socks off. Thank you for seeing in me what no one else has.

For Julie, who I can walk to the ends of the earth with. You open up my heart all the way back to my child-hood. You make me feel like I just drank champagne. And now I can fly.

For April, who knocks me out with the truth, blasting a grenade through my flimsy logic. You are my cosmi-cally-faceted-huge-indigo-sapphire-surrounded-by-baguette-diamonds friend.

And a huge round of applause for David Hinds, for say-ing "yes." And everyone at Celestial Arts who held my hand, returned my phone calls, encouraged me and fed me lunch with large doses of laughter.

Table of Contents

Laughing
While Your Life Raft
Is Sinking

Having It All Is Asking for Nausea

ᖆ You can't have it all. If you try to have it all your hair falls out, the in-laws hate you and your husband begins an affair because you're out improving yourself at an Improv class followed by Jazzercise.

There's something inherently wrong with having it all. It implies that there is enough time in the day to give yourself a complete pedicure, help the kids with their new math that you don't understand and save the world from pollution. Then on Tuesday you can earn busloads of money being a Hollywood screenwriter or a best-selling author, then make a well-balanced meal from scratch and enjoy a stunningly provocative intellectual conversation with your lover right before you fall asleep. Oh. And right after dizzying sex that the kids won't hear on the other side of the bedroom wall.

See? It doesn't happen that way. There are gaping holes in this type of logic. I for one barely have time to pick up the litter on my own lawn, let alone save the planet from toxic annihilation.

Last night my doorbell rang during the escalating battle that accompanies every bedtime for my ten-year-old son. We've been doing this for a decade and we still don't have it right.

The doorbell rings at 8:40PM. It's an appeal for money by a twenty-year-old girl to clean up the earth's water. I said, "I'm putting my son to bed. This isn't a good time."

She says, "Do you want me to come back in a half hour?"

No, you can come back when hell freezes over and then we'll have plenty of water. I just say, "No, don't come back."

Then she says, "Don't you care about this?"

Then I lost it. "Do you have children?" I ask her. Instead of answering she spins on her heels, beating a hasty retreat.

Of course she doesn't have children! When I told her it was 9PM she said, "It isn't 9PM yet." That sounds like a person who will be nursing a beer with friends after bothering citizens to cough up money for clean water when I thought I already had this covered every time I send a check to the IRS.

No! I don't want to save the world at 9 o'clock at night; I just want to finish a sentence without being interrupted and read to my kid and be able

to kiss my husband once a day and have fresh
laundry to fold and an ability to pay the rent.

Is that asking too much? I realized I can't have
it all because I can't even stay awake long enough
to have it all. Or to finish a sentence without being
interrupted.

This is slowly dawning on me.

For some reason I think I can simultaneously
write my memoirs, a screenplay, a book of essays,
finish my short film, run my own photography
business and be a full-time bread-making, nurturing mother and sexy wife who knows how and
what to do in bed and also, by the way, be a stun-
ning conversationalist. Did I leave anything out?

And I can't. I can't have it all and I'm beginning
to see that I don't even want to have it all. It takes
far too much energy to maintain constant wit and
resourcefulness and daring and make the beds too
without getting a permanent eye twitch. I wish I
could get rid of the one I already have.

I am beginning to accept the reality of things
piled in stacks littering my life. Tall columns of
items that are meant to be sorted. Things I'll get to
later.

I need an assistant but I'm too cheap to get one.
I think I should do it all myself and that is ludicrous.
I am doing the work of three people now and not

finishing what I start as it is. What makes me think that I can now hire a person to help me? Because the stacks are getting bigger and I don't want to be swallowed up by them.

It's perfectly acceptable not to own Bally shoes and the latest-model Caravan, which my son insists we must have. I simply cannot maintain that much materialism without feeling like I'm being run over by a concrete high-rise. Worse than nausea it would probably kill me.

But I need to be alive for our vacation coming up.

My major achievement of the day was getting through to the park system to reserve a campsite for our Easter getaway. The other campsite I wanted was booked until October and this is March. It only made me want it more to hear that I couldn't get it for half a year. So I was willing to take my kid out of school just to reserve a rustic cabin clinging to a cliff above the ocean. Sound good? Get in line.

There are days when I can zoom through my work, making short shrift of the demands and get-ting most of my desk cleaned and a lot of people called back. But then something else always suffers like my son's science fair project or I've gotten carpish from too much caffeine and have done little more than wave at the man I decided to spend the rest of my life with because there just isn't time. To say nothing of not walking the dog enough and shirking the collection of dust balls littered throughout the house.

It is only now that I'm forty that I realize I can't have it all. I can have a small piece of the pie but I must refuse to inhale the whole pizza and end up looking for somewhere to spew.

I will focus on the fact that yesterday I planted pansies and petunias and I am immensely grateful for that.

And I should start interviewing for assistants so I can have help in living my life.

Being Ecstatic

ᴥ Ecstasy is the most misunderstood emotion there is. If you're too happy others suspect illegal drug use or worse, a mental aberration. Ecstasy is unwelcome in corporate America. That's why psychiatrists invented the Ecstasy drug—so their patients would have somewhere to turn while the shrinks took Wednesdays off to golf at Pebble Beach.

We didn't know we could just be ecstatic.

When I'm truly ebullient the no-funitis police come out in full force to check my exploding expanding spirit. Their faces are creased and furrowed, their eyebrows say, "You shouldn't be having this much fun." Their tone of voice breathes condescension. There must be something wrong with you if you're that happy, they sniff with their hooded eyes.

Yes. It takes courage to be ecstatic when everyone else around you is checking their mutual fund point spread. It takes guts to allow our frothy, foamy head of enthusiasm to rise and not be drowned out by the voices of no-funitis. "No Fun Ever!" their banners wail, pinned across the main streets of our towns.

You've seen them just like I have. Scalps knit in consternation over why spring in California is "cold" (oh please!) or how will they ever manage to get all three children off to soccer practice on time? If you have exciting news to impart they want you to consider that someone died doing that about a hundred years ago.

They aren't believers in ecstasy. They dump raw sewage on your brainpan and call it "conversation." It takes muscle and heart to stand up to the recreational rejecting and disapproving, to just blanket the bullshit and be a firm believer in fun. This way you won't get a tumor. And it's the only way to save the planet.

The furrowed faces think they know the answer and it's worrying hard about how to get the kid into Stanford and then how to pay for it and then does the husband still like me? So we wipe off our smiles and kick ourselves from behind, then ask others to do it for us.

People give up on ecstasy too soon. It hurts. I'm tired. It takes practice. What will the neighbors think? I don't have time. These are the excuses. Pretty lame.

"I don't have time for ecstasy" is my favorite. We're too busy unloading the dishwasher and answering our voicemail to remember ecstasy. It might hurt. The doctor would take away our Prozac.

My rules for maintaining ecstasy:

1. Drive around sourpusses who feed on the life-blood of those who laugh for a living. Like mosquitoes they suck you up and spit you out, glumly shouting, "It's easy for you to be happy, your husband helps with the childrearing."

2. Never travel in a confined space with severely afflicted no-funitis fans. This will permanently damage your enthusiasm gene.

3. When the urge to blast complaints arises in the throat as it surely will, cough hard to clear the obstruction and go buy yourself a milkshake.

4. Do what's important, not what is necessary. Instead of presoaking stains, go for a walk in the woods.

5. Maintain control over the insidious no-funitis patrol. Refuse to be sideswiped by their badly defeated oars in the river of life. Go around them and laugh as often as you can at them. They hate this.

6. Find friends who marvel at your soul! These people move fast and are light-footed. Wet blankets will try to trip you up and smother your

dreams in their sodden embrace. Look else-
where!

7.   Practice enthusiasm when good fortune settles
on others. Even if you want to scratch their eyes
out, don't. Applaud their gain. Ask questions
and find out how it happened. Fairy dust will
fall on you.

8.   Get quiet and listen to the beating of your own
soul. Don't get up to see what's going on in the
refrigerator. Stay rooted on the couch. Don't
speak. Listen. Stare at the cobwebs, the ant on
the floor, the crumb it's carrying away. You'll
hear answers. Or people yelling. Sometimes it's
both. This is good.

9.   It's okay to be pissed off. Just don't make it a
permanent part of your wardrobe. Anger ages
you. It churns up the blood and whips it into
poisonous venom. Don't stay there too long.
Get out! Look into a baby's eyes and get over
yourself.

10. Run away for the weekend. Come back with a
new attitude. Don't come back until you stop
snarling.

That's it. Now do it.

Dog People

∽ I love dog people. They allow slobbering tongues to graze over their designer finery and dirty jagged claws to drag along their Evan Picone stockings and dry-clean-only dress-up pants.

I became a dog person last year when I realized cats are too aloof, unappreciative of the vet bills and isolationists at heart. I wanted an animal to love me, to thrill at my steps upon the porch, to greet me in gratitude every morning upon awakening. Maybe even perform some stupid dog tricks for guests. I wanted companionship and cuddling, sort of like having a new lover. One is starry eyed and gleeful, sparkly over the freshness.

A gong went off in my head. It said, go to the pound now! On a Wednesday afternoon at 4:15 PM I was thinking more of a cocktail and putting my feet up. But no. The gong was insistent.

"I'm going down to the pound, just to look," I calmly informed Michael.

"Really, can we go right now?" Wolfe asked.

Michael reached for his wet blanket. "It's too late now—let's wait until July when we need something new to perk us up."

I'm glad I didn't listen.

"No, no, I'm just going look at what they have and check it out. Don't worry, we won't come back with a dog." Yeah right.

Wolfe was flying to the car and in minutes we were walking into the cleanest animal shelter I'd ever seen, greeted by smiles and hearty hellos. Hey, we were home now. Sandra, the "adoption specialist," gave us a leash and let us loose in the kennels. It was all over after that.

Our eyes met those of a white poodle with blue bows on his poofy crown of hair. It was the badly cut Afro over his dark beseeching eyes that melted our hearts. "Get these bows out of my hair and give me back my dignity!" he telegraphed. We ran to the cage and stuck our fingers through the grill. He licked our hands with what began as tentative enthusiasm and quickly became a kissing frenzy. He was our dog.

On his cage was an introduction card: "Hi, my name is Cyrano. I have some problems, but I'm energetic and smart. I'm 3½ years old." Well, who wouldn't have problems with blue bows in his hair? He looked emotionally distraught, banged around maybe, abandoned by his family.

"Let's just peek at the other dogs for a second."

We walked through the prison corridor of

caged animals. There were only two other inmates to choose from. We were drawn to a chocolate Lab until our poodle started barking when we acted too interested in his neighbor. Then he went into desperation mode. He performed a stupid dog trick in front of us. Standing and walking on his hind legs, his face said, "Look at me. I'll be your floor show for the rest of my life." That cinched it.

We wanted to bring him home that day just like we said we wouldn't, but instead we put a hold on him until Michael could come down and see him. Wolfe said, "What about his name? Cyrano is a yucky name."

"We'll change it," I said.

"I want to name him Fluffy," he said with finality. Having never named a dog, he was pumped up with the importance of the moment. What could I say? I wanted to name him Foo Foo.

Fluffy was upset that we were leaving him in the kennel. He looked outraged: "What do you mean you're leaving me? I'm supposed to be going with you! I'm sure you're making a grave mistake." He barked at us.

Dog people everywhere know how I felt. Like opening up each cage and letting the English setter mix and rottweiler/boxer out to run free. But they

have to find good homes first so they don't multi-
ply and run ragged through the streets.

I walked out of there, proud and pleased to
adopt my orphan, to give a warm home to a crea-
ture who had been abandoned by his former own-
ers because "he was possessive and didn't fit in"
with their newer dogs. Our Fluffy? Who just looked
like he needed a better haircut and some love to
take the degradation out of his eyes?

I am irrationally in love with Fluffy. We spend
more time together than I do with both my main
squeeze and my only begotten son. He looks totally
bereaved when I go off just to grocery shop. He is
a master at guilt-inducing stares designed to repro-
gram my schedule for the afternoon. Just the way
he stands in the hallway as I'm about to leave,
screams, "No, you can't be abandoning me again.
You wouldn't leave me unattended once more
would you?" He's so mad at me, he can't even say
good-bye. I have found him moments later, still
standing in the same spot, pointing sorrowful eyes
at the front door, when I discover I've forgotten my
car keys and have to come back to retrieve them.

The worst revenge he can come up with is to
forage in either Wolfe's room or the garbage for
some half-eaten KitKat or abandoned avocado peel
to leave out on the Persian carpet in the living

room. He doesn't even like avocados but he knows that this is the equivalent of screaming obscenities at me without saying a word. He continues to do it even though he always gets in trouble and is rebuked for being a "baaaad dog!"

He only does this when he's really mad. He starts cowering the instant I see him after his open display of rage. He does not greet me joyfully, long curly-haired poodle ears flying beside him. The stench of guilt surrounds him; he knows he's done "baaaad" but he couldn't help it—he was left behind again! Damn it!

Fluffy has the kind of eyes that make me change my travel plans and decide to bring him along as carry-on baggage when I board the plane. I refuse to be daunted by the size restrictions of those tiny plastic kennels that only a Chihuahua would fit in. I was turned around by a spiffy piece of luggage called a "sherpa bag." Fluffy would ride in the zippered bag just like a video camera or laptop computer—he was coming with us and did not have to mope when the big suitcases came down out of the hall closet.

Only another dog person understands why I talk to Fluffy, call him a "baby" and generally act like a premenopausal woman in need of a last fling at motherhood. But this is much easier; I don't

have to use a breast pump or pay for his college
education. All I have to do is keep him from biting
little children, feed him Kibble and the occasional
bits of lung log and douse him with love.

Fluffy sniffs out the dog lovers from the less
enlightened riff raff. When potential clients come
calling at the front door he barks voraciously until
the intruders are invited in, then, since I seem to
like them, he figures out that they are not here to
rob or maim us. Then he begins to cajole them,
"Let me up on the couch, I want to cuddle with
you." The dog people are delighted. They fuss over
him, talk to him like he's a person and invite him
onto their thighs. We have a very pleasant conversation about how wonderful dogs are and forget all
about wedding photography. Fluffy preens in their
laps, tries to lick them from inches away and acts
like he'd just as soon become their newest family
member.

The world is divided into two kinds of people.
Dog people and those who do not relish cuddling
with a canine and being licked with a dog breath
tongue. The latter arrives at my house and looks
pained when Fluffy jumps on their pressed jeans,
asking to be cradled on the couch. He won't take
no for an answer, he's sure he can convert them to
dog-personhood if only he could lick their eye-

glasses. He insists on jumping between their knees as they look at my photography. They shoo him away and look at me with the whites of their eyes suggesting that I put him away—now.

These people are not dog people. They do not like dogs or dog hair or slippery tongues and they tell themselves rather proudly that they're allergic to dogs. I silently decide that perhaps photographing their wedding wouldn't be a rollicking good time. Maybe I should leave the date open for a dog lover.

Yesterday a dog person explained how she thought she was allergic to dogs until she got one and lived with him for two weeks. "I got used to him and my sniffles went away!" she said exuberantly. So even the allergy excuse can be kicked to shreds.

Even though I am a dog person I still make time for being a mother of a human child, a wife who doesn't act so wifey, a sister, a daughter, a lover, a photographer, an author, a friend, a filmmaker. But when everyone I know is too busy, my dog stands beside me or falls asleep on my thigh. He's always there for me.

Dog people. I am now a proud member of that species.

Life in a Nutshell

ᏍᏫ *Marriage:* Being married is a lot better than surfing bars looking for a good lay. It's much better to go to bed mad at the husband because he fell asleep while you were baring your soul. And not your ass.

Children: Right after your hip bones crack open and you deliver a fully formed human being, the thought arises that this child will need a college education and the keys to your car. Then you cover the critter with kisses and get into a warm bath and marvel at how miraculous it is that you reached into heaven and pulled out a baby from between your own thighs. That is way cooler than anything Lee Iaccoca has done this year.

Sex: I wish I had more time for sex but it's hard to get my kid to fall asleep before his parents do. Somehow the idea of silk teddy sex on the other side of the same wall as my own flesh and blood's bedroom makes my horniness disappear down a tunnel marked PARENTHOOD. Before having kids you want sex all the time; after having kids you just want to stare at a wall and not be disturbed. Or be able to read *People* magazine uninterrupted.

Meditation: I have figured out why I meditate. I really like the sound of the refrigerator humming at 5 in the morning and it doesn't ask me for an allowance or demand to know where its shoes are. I like peace and quiet and getting up at the crack of dawn is the only way to get it. After a while I can't feel my hands anymore. I'm not even sure I have thumbs.

Dying the Roots: I decided to avoid looking like the school principal and started dying my hair. I was beginning to look dried out and lackluster. My gray hair proves nothing except that I'm too cheap to get it done by a professional and look good. Even glamorous. If other women think it's groovy to be gray, let them be gray. Besides, I only have to smell that stuff Bianca puts on my head to transform me into a blonde, I don't have to touch it. Only professionals should be allowed to do root jobs. I learned this after I let my husband bleach my hair a lovely lemon meringue color.

Domestic Servitude: I would rather wade through dustballs the size of Montana and eat popsicles naked than vacuum the floor and clean out the refrigerator. I'm sort of a slob but no one knows it because my husband is neat except when he stockpiles magazines and garage sale items in the basement. I never learned the beauty of dusting and am now just barely acquainted with rinsing out the dishes after the last three meals.

Creativity: I get foul-mouthed and crabby when I can't do anything more creative than hang up the clothes to dry. Whenever I get depressed I go out in my garden and talk to the dahlias. They respond by growing actual flowers. Then I realize that I have to write immediately or shoot some film with my camera. Moving makes the blood flow better and I'm less likely to reach for a cocktail.

Money: When I worry about paying the rent I become a two-horned beast who isn't much fun while my kid exclaims, "Look what I can do with my Mario game!" I want to be debt free but the credit card statements arrive and convince me that I'm not. I'm learning how to tighten my belt but that means not going to restaurants. Michael is going to have to grow up and get a real job.

Abundance 101—When Bankruptcy Looms: I just tallied up what we owe everyone. It was so sobering I can barely stand up without a scotch in my hand. I am deciding that even debt cannot get me down. I will rise above this and enjoy what I have already. Nice underwear and a Hasselblad that's actually paid for. Also my child is a live-in guru who I kiss too much, but try not to, and I have good sex with my husband even though I'm mad at him for not paying back all the bills.

Therapy: I used to think that therapy was for rich overfed yuppies who didn't have any best friends. But it's actually helped me to talk to a trained professional who listens to me and doesn't tell me her problems. Sometimes friends are too quick to point out that you're fucking your life up and then they leave because they're really busy and have to go back to work. Therapists can't escape. They have to sit there and listen even if they want a cigarette really badly. You pay them to be nice to you and also to ground the shit out of you. I like that in a therapist. This way I might even grow up.

Dogs: I am with my dog more than I am with the other humans who live here. My dog and I spend hours together while my son and husband have other things to do. I like my dog because he talks with his tail and curls up next to my thighs when I'm sitting on the couch. When I leave him behind and lock the front door he looks at me like I've just pointed a rifle at him. He acts like I should never leave home without him because it would be a lot more fun if he came along.

Work: I like shooting weddings because I wait patiently in the folds of God's robe for magic to happen in these huge moments that flit by in seconds. I get out of the way when God surges up my pointer finger, tripping the shutter at a sixtieth of a second, capturing emotion on film forever. They write me a big check and let me take pictures all day, which I like doing anyway, and then tell me I did a great job before they even see the photographs. It's really only work when I lift the camera bags into the car and have to deal with rich mothers stamping their feet because I wasn't able to stop the UPS strike single-handedly.

The Afterlife: Catholics know how to live it up when it comes to dying. They give you a big party and throw lots of prayers and flowers at you. The saints I've read about were always happy about dying. Flying through time zones and never paying taxes sounds great to me. I'm rather looking forward to it.

Yoga After 15 Years of Abstinence

❧ I thought I'd amble on down to the local yoga center and do some stretching after a dry spell of fifteen years. I had no idea I'd be sweating like a sumo wrestler, close to blackout and wondering when an hour and a half would be up. Whew. I'm winded just thinking about it.

A decade and a half ago I told my sister that I was doing yoga and she scoffed, "Oh, that's not strenuous like running is." She ran, of course, and was never asked to balance on one leg while wrapping the other leg around her left ear.

Christina, the walking billboard of the class, looks like she was born doing yoga and has never stopped. Or has ever eaten a shred of red meat or a Snicker bar. I was in awe. I tried not to look at her as I wobbled on one leg holding up 145 pounds while negotiating the other leg towards the ceiling. And then she would say, "Look behind you at the wall and grasp your ankles while standing on your knees." I realized that she meant for us to look at the wall with our heads thrown back all the way to

L.A. and between our knees in the cobra position
without blacking out. Whenever I thought, oh this
isn't too bad, I was doing it wrong and would catch
a glimpse of another student looking like Parma-
hansa Yogananda himself.

Is it really possible to kiss my toes with my forehead while pressing my thighs into my spare tire?

My friend Kate, who was responsible for getting
me down there, is a yoga instructor and even she
was sweating buckets. So it wasn't just me. This is
hard! Good thing I'm in a class because I would
never do it alone; I'd rather have a cup of coffee
and a long walk and a nice read by the fireplace I
don't have.

But I do feel awake and alive. As one woman
said to me at the break, "You feel as though you've
earned the rest of the day." And how. I feel like I
should receive a medal in bravery just for attempt-
ing to wrap my arms around the back of my legs
while lifting my haunches into the air without
expiring. And I thought aerobics was hard. I also
thought playing the stockmarket and making cold
calls was hard until this morning at about 9:30
when I realized I'd never be the same again after
trying to wedge my body into unnatural positions
and feel the blood flowing into my heart like I
never have before.

I was inspired by all the lithe bodies I saw and how their age was not registered on their faces. With a hard butt and a fluid attitude you can surely conquer the world. And more importantly, flog the inner demons that compress our souls like stomped on doormats.

I accomplished a soul-baring hour and a half this morning, watching my body in that mirror, concentrating on the worry lines between my eyebrows, about to collapse from the lifting, stretching, breathing nonstop. No time off for good behavior.

And I'm glad I went and I'm even going back again for more challenge. I don't feel so clogged up and comatose.

This yoga class is changing my life. I just know it.

That is the most demanding thing I've done since pushing Wolfe out of my body ten years ago. It's high time I sweat like a sumo wrestler again.

The Jail of Jealousy

೦೦ I was between a rock and a hard place. Being scrutinized by piggy eyes that told me, "Stop being who you are right now." I was telling a mother about her daughter, a girl in Wolfe's class who I dearly love for her spirit, her mind, her questions, her articulation and her sweet face with the blue almond eyes and tinkling laughter.

"I love her!" I told her mother. Spittle flew out of her mouth when she answered, "You love everyone!" in a diminishing tone of voice.

So did Jesus. Like that's a character flaw.

"It takes courage to be a joyful person."

She answers, "Going around being a bubbleheaded joyful person is not the way to be."

I had fallen in love with her daughter after spending three days with her on a field trip with 87 fourth graders. She wasn't among the mothers who had been there. She spits out at me, "My daughter said that you said children are smarter than adults."

They are smarter. And I'm sick and tired of boring people over forty who hasten to defend that we aging, jaded, older people who have lost the joy in life have something to teach these young ones who have such big spirits, untethered by mortgages and what other people will think. There was this woman who does not like how I laugh and had just made the comment "Push the button and you laugh" as she pressed her fist into my shoulder, says to me, "I don't want her to know all the bad stuff that's happening in the world."

I told her, "Children give you a different per-spective on things."

"They give you a different perspective on mur-der?" she spat.

She did not want to hear how her daughter was special presumably because it was me telling her. She was mad. (She had just come from a bidding war at our school's annual silent auction. This is where parents bid on weekends in Mendocino and cabins without electricity in the mountains which they could just pay for without benefit to the school, but the money goes to our computer fund so it's all good clean fun. But not when the bidding comes dangerously close to blows.)

I'd had enough of her wisecracking meanness. I was casually curious as to how this woman had raised such an excited, beautiful, bright and gifted little girl. She didn't even know her own kid. How could she when she wasn't willing to acknowledge how this girl's spirit had touched my heart?

Later I thanked her daughter for the lovely note she gave me for coming on the class field trip. I cried when I read it.

Thank God Michael came to rescue me with the announcement, "Wolfe's kindergarten teacher is here with her baby!"

Here's what I learned. It's better to walk away from evil than to stay right there and be hit in the face with its flying spittle. I am no longer interested in being friends with anyone who wishes that my joy would just go away and not be in their face so much. I am so weary of women who don't want to have any fun at all that I could just scream but instead I'll walk away or just say, "Next!" It isn't beautiful or nurturing to be told "NO" to my spirit overflowing with excitement.

And I am no longer interested in being flayed by parasitic tongues that want me to stop being myself and listen to their laundry list of complaints about life.

NO. Not when I can laugh with ten-year-old girls, try new adventures and speak my mind.

I am not afraid to be myself anymore. I am not giving up laughter so that some pinch-faced person suffering from no-funitis can have the floor and bore me. I am finally free from the disemboweling I used to take on a regular basis from people who wanted me to stop laughing because they weren't having any fun and, damn it, why should I when they weren't?

And I am very tired of parents who do not listen when I tell them how special their children are and to wake up and know that about them.

Children are smarter. They haven't gotten jaded yet. They still get excited over what they love. Adults devolve into this pooh-pooh stance on life that it isn't seemly to be silly or have fun. We must settle into a paunch and assume the position of a person beaten with the rocks of reality. We must suffer and make the car payments. Why not get rid of the car if that's the way you feel?

After seeing Gaelyn, my friend the Zen priest, in her world of meditation in the woods amidst a community of spiritual seekers of simplicity, even for that brief two minutes of time that I got to look at her and see the blue of her eyeballs expand out into the universe, I get how we don't need all the luxuries. She doesn't have any and she's still laughing.

So here it is. The experience is better than the Ford Cherokee. Laughter in the bosom is better than a leather-lined Lincoln. A kiss on the lips from your kid is better than sumptuous fabrics draping your body and shouting to the world that you've made it.

You haven't made it until a child tells you that they love you. That is true wealth. Everything else is just money in the bank.

When a child loves you the world is right. A child's love reaches past the dark demons of your soul and makes you whole again. They haven't forgotten how to love, they who are so freshly from God. They are angels come to teach us and we will hear their wisdom only if we can shut our fat egos and listen to their soft wings unfolding, telling us to laugh and love. That is always the answer.

Always.

Living with Lice

᠊ᡣᠥ It's been three months now that a scourge has been incubating in our household. So I'm cutting off Wolfe's hair and perhaps even vacuuming. I can't take it anymore.

Personally I feel that it was our family alone who set off a citywide lice epidemic. He's had the critters since last August and we've endured burning chemicals on our tender scalps, complete hose-downs of our entire wardrobes and still the insidious vermin keep coming. I'm ready to slit my wrists. I'm going to my film class tonight where I could ask a student to film me doing it. Wrist slitting may be avant garde experimental cinema but it makes me want to throw up.

But back to bugs. Namely tiny, clinging, sticky lice that invade one's demeanor and domain. When I think of exactly where each one of us has laid their hair shafts on sofas, pillows, each other, clothing, I cringe. One must scour every surface, destroy every egg, comb every last hair follicle. It smacks of anal-retention hygiene, this constant combing, shampoo that smells like Agent Orange and lethal hair spray to be used only on those surfaces that cannot be washed with boiling water and powdered grenades. I'm at my wit's end.

April warned me about this last summer. I cockily assured her that I needn't wash all my 100% cotton bedding, it would shrink in the dryer! She laughed. "No," she quietly insisted, then she pounded the table with her fist and yelled, "Napalm everything in your house!"

I didn't listen. I thought I could do this alone. Without God, an army of RID and a can of RID spray attached to my belt in a holster. I told myself I would vanquish and destroy this microscopic speck and demand it to be banished from my underwear, my castle, my natural bristle brushes! I was a fool. And now I an combatting a virus, like syphilis that strikes unawares, as my kid cozies up to computer headphones at school, as he tousles with another infected child, or as he reinfects himself on towels that have not been properly deloused in his own home.

I fervently took him to Sunny's house to have his hair cut. She is a saint among children's hair stylists and a goddess among lesser beings. She wouldn't allow me at her beauty parlor. "The girls have a fit!" 'The girls' are her co-workers, hair maven specialists who cut only adults' hair and we adults never get lice. Except when our kids so sneakily give it to us and we wonder for the twenty-fifth time in fifteen minutes why we keep scratching our scalps. I'm gonna have to get serious here. Nightly inspections of hair parted with fingertips and X-rayed with blood-shot eyes scouring for sticky specks of lice offspring.

This is the fourth or fifth time I've rubbed the caustic shampoo into Wolfe's tender scalp, coating each of his too long hairs with pungent syrup. It drops in globs on his shirt, the chair, my clothes. I sat meditating in my bathrobe last week and sud-denly the acrid smell of RID wafted up my nose and into my peaceful trance. There just isn't any-where that's safe anymore. It would be lovely to leave home with instructions to bomb the critters out to some qualified personnel who take care of such things, but I have to do it and I'm the only one in the house who understands the sheer terror of this pinhead-sized bug living in our midst.

Wolfe's hair is so napalmed now that cutting it off will release him of brittle bleached hair shafts that stand up like straw. I just paid a hair color pro-fessional to tint my hair the exact shade of blonde that makes Michael feel like he's having an affair with his own wife, so the thought of delousing my tresses with toxic acid is not sitting well with me. Why couldn't this happen before I spent the fifty bucks? But no, lice creep into your worst nightmare and make you wish you no longer even had hair on your head. Believe me, I'm ready to shave mine off.

Michael casually mentions that his head itches and I'm off and running for the Raid, I mean RID, wondering will I have to do it too? And knowing that I will since we sleep so close together he can't inhale without me knowing about it.

I was happy before lice visited me. I thought, we're finally enjoying life and paying back bills, anticipating new endeavors—and boom, lice crossed my path, snuggled up in bed with me and won't leave, like annoying relatives who decide to move in after their three-week vacation living on your sofa.

I blithely told Wolfe's best friend's father, "Oh, we're done with lice" when he inquired after the safety of our boys sleeping together in a tent for a Boy Scout overnight after my child had so recently been infested with lecherous lice. Meanwhile, my child was crawling with them and I didn't even know.

Just writing this makes every hair on my body itch. It's time for my next treatment of hair care from hell, malathion shampoo guaranteed to kill everything in its path. That is, unless you miss one little nit and it's nesting in your fresh sheets right now.

Get out the hand grenades—this is war.

Home Shopping Saves the Planet

∾ All you have to do is buy a tiny bird feeder which could easily be bashed with your foot and your sex life will improve, your kids will learn about nature and you'll be protecting the environment. Just watch the home shopping channel and your life will dramatically improve overnight. For $14.95 plus $4 shipping you too can be happy.

Wolfe is home sick. So I check what he's watching on TV while he recuperates. First it was some teenage show that I didn't know the name of and then it was *Happy Days* and then it was the home shopping channel. A well-fed sixtyish looking guy is sitting there with a huge diamond ring on his finger which he keeps twirling so that the diamond is facing the television audience, and he's expounding on just why this little bird feeder will change your life. My God, there's no other way to improve your children's grades and your sex life all in one day! Just buy this lovely genuine imitation plywood home for hummingbirds and your life will take off. And notice how gaily it's painted. It will cheer you up when you want to ring someone's neck. When you're about to go bankrupt. It's the answer to all your problems. Stop what you're doing and get on the phone now before they run out. Your life will never be the same.

Just when you thought it was safe to watch TV again because *Married with Children* is going off the air you find out that a bird feeder you have to put together yourself is for sale and will make a mountain out of your molehill life. How have we ever been able to survive without shopping on TV?

Next we have a lovely plastic machine that rolls your pennies for you. The fluidity of the pennies rolling into stacks makes me want to get on the phone and order it now. It's really the money itself that attracts me. Would they send $50 worth of coins so I can play with them?

By now Wolfe and I are rolling on the floor. Our lives will be transformed overnight if we only have this birdfeeder in our world. And more importantly we'll be saving the planet.

I like the sex part too. By the time Michael gets home I'll be a changed woman. Especially if I order it Federal Express.

Drowning in Trash

⍦ I can't stand it anymore. I'm drowning in little bits of paper gathered and squirreled away from the last fifteen years.

I like to blame Michael for all of this. He's the one who can't seem to part with anything he has personally touched from the last millennium and he is storing it all in our basement. I went down there today and wanted to set a match to it. Bits of information on pieces of paper will be why I run naked down the street yelling obscenities completely sober. It is time to take action and it means throwing things out.

I have two guys to deal with in this scenario. Wolfe, my only begotten son, has learned how to save everything from Michael, a master at finding worth in a pile of papers he hasn't touched since the McCarthy era and he wasn't even around then. He has crap left over from his parents' former marriage, like the paper their divorce settlement was written on and their respective grandparents' newspaper clippings that prove they were important in their communities. Just the kind of reading you want to do after a fifteen-hour work day when just sitting and staring into space seems like an effort.

I want to start over and have a life again, not just shuffle piles of newspapers and magazines from upstairs to the death knell of those stacks in the basement. Once the offensive items are stored in the basement they are no longer needed by anyone—until I decide to throw them out when a torrent of objections is raised so harshly you would think that I had just suggested killing our dog with my bare hands. Who, incidentally, I spend more time with than any other family member mostly because he doesn't collect anything in the basement. People say pets are a lot of work, but I know the truth. It's harder to take care of stacks of paper in the basement and the humans that stockpile them than any dog ever thought of being.

I'm thinking of decorating the basement in an early sledgehammer motif.

I will not enlist the help of my family, who will resurrect reasons why the free toys that come with a kids' meal will one day be a collectable item and will pay for my son's education at Harvard. All I have to do is be willing to look at the offensive article until this magical moment in history long after he has graduated from a public college, gotten married and had three kids. Oh, I forgot. Wolfe once told me, "I'm not having kids because I just want to play golf." Implying that my future grandchildren would take too much time away from the perfection of his swing.

I have a sneaking suspicion that all the discarded toys in the basement that are now layered with dust will never be more useful than when they were first purchased. That is why I am going to remove the piles of forgotten memorabilia to make room for the scraps of paper I'm trying my damnedest to coordinate above ground in the main living area.

Once I give away the magazines Michael hasn't read for the last ten years, I am sure that he won't ask me where the May 1989 issue of *Motorland* is. I am positive that he is not going to research our checkbook stubs from the last century in an attempt to excavate some obscure expenditure in case we get audited. And even the IRS thinks looking at records from the first half of the millennium is a waste of time. They usually want to see more recent pieces of paper that make up the bulk of my decorating decisions.

So it's decided. I am not going to slit my wrists. I'm just gonna have a garage sale and not invite the rest of my family, who would struggle with departing shoppers as they carry away precious artifacts,

insisting that they return the item just purchased
'cuz that amazing shoeshine machine that weighs
200 pounds and which I've been stubbing my toes
on for the last two years shouldn't have been in the
pile to be sold.

They'll never notice that all their one-of-a-kind
treasures have been tagged and removed from the
cellar.

And then I'll be able to breathe again.

Inside My Skin

Flirting
Made My Neck Hair
Stand Up

၆ဟ He was looking at me the way a starling watches
the sun rise. Starting at my feet, moving past my
ankles, sliding along my thighs, up over my stomach, stopping at my breasts, not caring that I saw
his eyes lingering there, and into my eyes. Not letting a square inch of me go unnoticed.

I felt naked.

It took my breath away and gave it back to me
in a whisper. My brain was on holiday as his wry
smile danced across his face. I wanted to hug him.
But I couldn't do that now when I was breathing
the air that surrounded him in a tantalized way. His
eyes met mine after traveling up the length of my
life in bodily form.

I hardly knew him and now we were face to
face in a parking lot staring at one another across
asphalt and wedding bands. My words stuck in my
throat and I became warm around the hairline of
my boundaries that suddenly sprang up like

weeds. I wanted to hold him right there on the
asphalt and I couldn't. We're both married to other
people. Happily married, remember? How could
this happen in suburbia outside a grocery store
while loading bags of food into my car? And why
would it happen with him, whom I had never been
alone with?

His hands were in his pockets now. His eyes
met mine like an anchor thrown from a ship after
an ocean voyage. He said simply, "You cut your
hair." No greeting after two years, just a statement
which immediately made me like him more for
having dispensed with the formality of "hi, how are
you's" and "what are you up to's." I was rooted to
the pavement and didn't want to pry myself off.

I just wanted to look at him longer and not be
interrupted with words. Watching the way he
walked, how he moved his hands which were hidden from view, hiding his feelings. If I could just
see his hands I would know exactly how he felt, but
after that look that ran the length of my body in
several lifetimes he wasn't going to reveal much
now. Oh yes. We remembered we were married.

He was innocently suggesting that we get
together for dinner to discuss a book idea I had.
But the book didn't matter now. I had been hit with
a bolt of reality deeper than a book proposal. The

soul-searing slash on my heart said run the other
way if you want to stay married.

I thought about his wife at home waiting for
him to bring the groceries back for dinner. Whatever he brought home would be made into dinner
on the spot. She was not a leftover kind of person. I
had wanted to be her new best friend and now I
was surveying her one and only man like the person who draws lines around a property with one of
those surveying telescopes. Just what had happened
here was sweeping my ardor under a nice conservative statement of let's pretend this didn't happen
even though we both know it did. No one will ever
know except us, and we can pretend that it didn't
happen either after a while. But it was too raw and
honest to ever forget no matter who we were married to. It had happened. It was the kind of look
that changes lives and moves mountains.

In another lifetime maybe.

But not in this one. I was knocked off my square
of concrete, shaken up and rattled. We saw the fire-
works and after catching our breath at the beauty,
backed off. We were looking over our wedding rings
at the grass on the other side of our marriages.

Later, when Michael and I went to his house
dressed as a married couple visiting friends, his
hands were in his pants again. When I walked in

his front door he didn't turn around, kept snapping off the asparagus tips for dinner like he was too busy to talk. I let him get away with it and rhapsodized over their new remodeling. But I was miffed that he hadn't even looked at me yet. It wasn't at all like it had been in the parking lot. In fact he wasn't even the same person—where did he go so fast?

He was not going to let that part of him out again. And I wasn't going to let him know how much his look had reached my soul. I regarded him over the bright and shiny new fixtures of chrome and granite in their new kitchen and swallowed a sip of wine.

Thank God for brevity and silence.

Stark Naked

 My neighbors know me better than my intimates. They see me walking to the curb at 7AM in my bathrobe that parts and reveals my naked legs that stretch all the way to Anchorage into my underpants. Then I casually say "hi" to my neighbor the Stanford professor, who has heard me do unspeakable things in the five years I've lived next door to him. I'll tell you about them anyway.

He's heard me scream at my kid like I was gonna beat him up but, of course, never did. It's much more ineffective to yell like a banshee with its bazoo on backward than to sit down quietly and explain in detail just why he should clean out the kitchen bomb he concocted in the microwave. Sputtering and stupefied rambling follows my inept attempts to control the contents of my spice drawer from becoming yet another experiment in fourth grade chemistry.

My neighbors have also heard me having sex in my bedroom when I didn't realize their children were using my nice smooth driveway as a skateboard ramp on the other side of my bedside window. Maybe that's why his ex-wife moved out and labeled me an unfit mother and told her child, my kid's best friend, that he couldn't play over here anymore. Gee, doesn't anyone ever have sex anymore?

My neighbors see me dancing on the sidewalk on Christmas, walking my dog in my bathrobe too far from my house to still be considered sane and encouraging my child to burn up a cardboard box just so I could get it on film for the short I'm doing about a nine-year-old boy's perspective on life, starring my kid. I explained it all to the police officer when he showed up the next morning to inquire about the burnt box that looked like it was a bomb threat to the neighborhood.

These are things that I would never intentionally do to my best friends. But my neighbors get to see me doing all sorts of unsavory acts like bending over too far in my miniskirt when I can't stand the sight of those weeds in my marigolds. Speaking of which, one of my neighbors sees me stark naked as I cross my deck to get to our outdoor claw-foot bathtub for a nice relaxing soak. I thought her boyfriend would enjoy the view but he doesn't often see the light of day, so I have to limit my baths until after dark. What a bother.

One thing I am eternally grateful for is that the ninety-year-old lady next door is deaf. That way she can never tell when the Doors or Jimi Hendrix decide to have a concert in my living room. The professor on the other side hasn't complained yet and he just became a millionaire. Maybe Jim Morrison had something to do with it. The professor was doing his research on his front porch while the Doors belted it out from over here.

I pray that my neighbors will continue to put up with me. If they do I will repay them with my homegrown tomatoes. With a side of Mick Jagger.

New York Gal
Does California

೧ Ya just can't take the New York outta me. I've survived twenty glacial winters trying to walk upright in blasts of gale force winds that made me grip the corners of buildings to avoid blowing away. One hundred fifteen inches of snow every year gave me an Ice Follies approach to life. Which is nothing all that serious because in the next snowstorm you won't be able to see or drive your car. After living here for eighteen years I'm still not a Californian.

I can't be a Californian. I could never say, "Oh, we're having such awful weather!" during a sprinkle of fresh rain that lasts for minutes and not months because I remember slipping on icy sidewalks wearing a short skirt and then having wet underwear for the rest of the day.

California largely does not have weather. The soft breezes turn to gentle rain when winter arrives here and everyone gets worried that it will flood. I'm just pleased that I don't have to water my lawn.

A New York winter is met with frantic searching for galoshes and nailing down anything you own that could blow away in a blizzard. Winter rat cars replace the ones that haven't been eaten through the quarter panels by street salt that keeps the pavements from becoming skating rinks.

Every spring I am ecstatic, marveling at how my tiny tomato plants will blow up into gargantuan bushes that feed whole families. I plant them in April when people in New York are still braving the snow. They have to wait until June to plant theirs. Here, the frost is over and I'm planting poppies, marigolds and impatiens in March!

I went back to New York for my twenty-year high school reunion. When I stepped off the plane I noticed my tan blaring in the November white-knuckle wind and realized that the time for getting tans in New York was three months past. I looked out of place.

But I still have my accent.

And now my son, who pronounces words just like I do, can't even understand me. I say, "Papa has to go to work," and Wolfe says, "I thought you said Papa has to go to New York."

I wish. I want to go back right now and swim in the lakes of the Adirondacks, drink New York State wine, eat the best blueberries on the planet and hard, sweet apples sparkling with flavor and wit. I only have pithy apples to eat here.

People in California have never heard an Upstate New York Finger Lakes accent. They don't know that everyone in Buffalo, Syracuse and Canandaigua sounds just like me. They think I'm from Wyoming, Missouri, Ohio even. It rubs me the wrong way to be accused of being a Midwesterner. New York has more magic in one snowflake than most states do in their entire borders. Okay, I'm belligerent. It's in my DNA, so sue me.

I'm proud of my New York in-your-face roots. I swear people laugh more in New York and continual teasing is the norm. Being offensive is more accepted in New York.

In California saying the truth can get you in trouble. When you get sick here you aren't supposed to tell anyone. If you have a cold people will jump back from your air space and demand fresh oxygen untainted by your infection.

People are more polite here, although I'm not. Just this morning Wolfe asked me, "Why do you always say 'shit this' and 'crap that' all the time?"

Do I have to watch my mouth so he doesn't fall into my style of expression? Swearing is the norm in New York. And saying what you mean when you think it. That is not accepted in California. People are too nice here and I don't believe them for a minute. Being negative is frowned upon and saying your true feelings is only done at a therapist's office, certainly not to your closest relatives in broad daylight. This bothers me. I'd rather let my feelings out than get a tumor keeping them in. Having a big mouth is better than getting cancer. And then people know where they stand with you.

Maybe that's what I'm mainly here for. To offend others.

There's a magic that comes from seeing the first snowfall every year twenty years in a row. But it's been almost entirely replaced by my fervor for liquid amber trees changing to orange and the daffodils blooming in January.

I even love the rain here because, as long as it's raining, I can luxuriate in flushing the toilet after every pee and my pansies and petunias are happy. When it rains I have an emerald green lawn. In a drought it looks like pissed-on dog dirt.

When I visit New York I rediscover that the trees are several yards taller than when I used to play under them. You never water your lawn there because it's always verdantly green and moist, leaving grass stains and wet marks on blue-jeaned butts after mere minutes of sitting on it. People hang out in their front yards in New York.

I was in shock when I discovered lawn sprinklers here. Pipes built into the dirt and set on a timer to expel water when it was told to! Why would anyone want to water their lawn? I was incredulous, and then summer came and our lawn died. I considered it an excessive use of water even without the drought. I forget that this is a desert under our feet here.

And I'm not afraid to mow my lawn here either. In California people think you must hire a gardener for such a plebeian task. We are much too busy taking over companies, learning Tae Kwon Do and finding ourselves to mow down tall grass. But I like doing it. It gives me a sense of accomplishment to see the lawn freshly cut and geometrically straight-edged like a ruler. I shear the borders on my hands and knees so the lawn will look like chiseled emeralds. I do this when my mind has turned to gruel and I need to feel dirt under my fingernails.

Speaking of front lawns, I have picnics on mine so I can stare at the oak tree at the corner. I do this without a permit and people walking by look flabbergasted. It's available real estate, why not use it?

We have an outside bathtub here that I can use year-round. An acquaintance came over and said, "Oh, a tub. That's nice for when the weather is good."

I like taking a hot bath when it's raining and the drops slither down between the apricot branches

onto my bare shoulders. She's not from New York
so she doesn't understand what the word "weather"
means. What would she know being born in Pen-
sacola?

California has lakes, rivers, mountains, the
desert, and the ocean, for God's sake, and still people complain about the traffic. What did they think,
they would have it all to themselves right after the
borders closed down when they arrived here? I just
can't get too upset with a state that is home to
Yosemite, Big Sur and San Francisco. What's up
with these people who whine about too many cars?
So get a job at home and stay off the roads. I've
been working at home for decades and now it's
suddenly "in" to have a home office. Even trendy. I
didn't know how "with it" I was because I usually
see myself as without it.

Speaking of trends, things are changing in California. Orange hair and mohawks are out. Bald
heads and nose piercing are in. Buddhism is on the
rise and I think even Catholics are enjoying a
comeback. We need our souls revitalized. It isn't
fun to sleep standing up or live while being dead.
Spiritualism is waxing. This may even be true in
New York where people smoke for a living.

Hardly anyone eats meat in California. But
double doses of scotch, Häagen-Dazs and

Ghirardelli chocolate are fine. I'm slightly irritated when people smoke here in the land of smoke-free restaurants, but in New York I just open a window and breathe normally. It doesn't bother me there.

The non-meat-eaters piously proclaim their love of animals, then scarf down multiple martinis with a chaser of Rocky Road ice cream bars. Then we all exercise with a fervor reserved for rock stars and TV evangelists and wear jazzercise clothes to the office. Sweatbands are tiresome, but we need our sun out here even though it's supposed to be bad for us. No one in New York worries about skin cancer because the sun doesn't shine there more than a few days a year.

No one within the borders of California drops by without a written invitation to visit. None of us are ever home unless we work at home and then we don't want to be bothered even answering the phone. In New York you welcome the sight of a friend showing up in a snowstorm to see you. Now you have someone to drink scotch with and join you in the cellar for an inspection of your frozen pipes.

Maybe in another twenty years I'll be a Californian, but I doubt it. If only because I'm too offensive.

Meager Money at Medi-Cal

෨ There's nothing that can't be solved while look-ing up into the tippy tops of swaying redwood tree boughs and praying with God. Even going to the Medi-Cal office and begging for a handout.

I had to go hug some redwood trees after bleat-ing for money at a government agency where my soul shriveled to the size of a walnut and my out-look grayed like whites washed with colors.

Hugging a redwood is like hugging a person. The bark gives against the weight of my body, the cushy spring of a tree trunk glides up above my head where the tops are flexible, bending gracefully in the breeze. Gazing up from the ground the branches look like they are conferring, and I see how it is possible to remain grounded at the roots while flexing to the blast of wind up top. And that's how it was at the Medi-Cal office.

But it was good for me to go. It made me see that smugness is an insidious social disease more prevalent than cancer. Anyone who thinks they are superior to their fellow man should spend a few hours trying to get public assistance from the state. It ain't a pretty sight.

Just when I thought it was safe to go naked without health insurance a hernia hovers in our future. Michael's intestines are not falling back into place like they used to. I wondered if it was because I kept telling him to get a day job.

He was just getting ready to start his Medi-Cal begging dance when he got hit with a gut-wrenching attack and I figured I better drive him down there. I rushed Wolfe along to get ready that morning and he asks me, "Could Papa die during the operation?" Then he hit his tender head on the car getting in.

So there we were, sitting on orange plastic chairs just like the kind in Greyhound bus stations.

I wish for just one hour Rush Limbaugh and several of his fundamentalist friends could come down to the public assistance waiting room and see for themselves why abortion is a good thing. It isn't right that women should have babies when they can't take care of them. I know that's hard for smug, white-collar fat pigs who chain-smoke and eat prime rib for a living to understand. Old white Republican men should not be allowed to decide what a woman can do with her body who is struggling to take care of herself at some menial job that she just lost. Without an education she's looking at a dishwasher job, or worse, a filing clerk who must wear pantyhose and pumps every day.

It's always the old Republican guys who have their Harvard and Yale educations safely behind them that yell the loudest about free rides for people who didn't get the benefit of rich parents and the right neighborhood. I shudder to think that these assholes, who can never feel the pain of a human being emerging whole from between their legs, are deciding the fate of abortion in Congress. They are men. Their opinion does not count about abortion. Just like women's opinions are never listened to when it comes to male birth control research. It's just so much easier for women to birth the babies, stay home barefoot and, only if necessary, take birth control pills. The men can continue to eat at Morton's Steak House, smoke cigars, wear Armani suits, pick pubic hairs off of Coke cans and decide what we women can and cannot do with our bodies. It would confuse our pretty little heads if we had to decide. Why don't they just dry out their pork bellies and die? I've had it with them.

I'm sitting there thinking, Do we really deserve free money? Aren't we too smart to succumb to this bureaucratic red-tape dance when there are

other people—who don't own a 1950 Cadillac con-
vertible worth $20,000—who need it more? I'm
squirming in discomfort but we have to pay for this
operation and all we have is credit. I've heard you
can't live on love these days. We need actual
money, dirty paper that it is.

Finally, after shouting down the receptionist
who "forgot" about us, we get to see the officer,
who wades through a stack of assistance papers
that we have to file, explaining how hard it will be
to establish our income when we don't work for
anyone but ourselves. This is not looking good.

"Who is the principal wage earner?"

We both point to me. I have been constantly
mentioning this fact to Michael for the last six
months so he will understand how much I don't like
it. Which is probably why he has the hernia. I'm the
one who works like a Clydesdale selling reprints
and albums while he stares into a computer monitor. I have called him "airy-fairy" too many times
this month. I am beginning to snap under the pressure of considering bankruptcy. I've suggested he
get a real job and not lean so heavily on my earning power. Going through the bill box feels like tip-
toeing through landmines. I'd like to get out of this
money crunch with all my limbs intact.

So here we are. The officer says to Michael,

"You have to sign a paper saying you're medically indigent."

"Indigent is such an ugly word," I say.

It's beginning to feel like a Woody Allen movie so we try to laugh through this. The stack of papers in front of me is too high. I am tempted to set a match to it and leave. They are gonna find out about the Cadillac and make us sell it to pay for a hernia operation. Maybe we should. But it's one of the only "things" I own that hoodwinks me into believing I'm rich when, in fact, I struggle to pay the rent. Driving the car is a state of mind. Is the officer gonna make me give that up? Oh man.

The officer is a nice guy, freshly back from a vacation in Hawaii. He was told that we would be "an easy case to process." When he discovers we are self-employed his eyes roll into his hairdo. It is not favorable that Michael is not "the principal wage earner."

"Just because I'm so damn bright we can't get help when we need it."

So much for being the leading loudmouth of the family who chases down money the most. Damn. I never played the supporting wife act and now this. Just because I didn't simper, "Oh honey, you make the money for all of us," I'm being punished now.

This is ridiculous. I don't want them delving into our assets, such as they aren't, considering the fact that driving a monstrous piece of black metal and chrome is extraneous. But that's how they do it down there.

Assets and income. It doesn't matter how much we owe—that's our problem.

It's work to juggle all these forms flashing before my eyes as the officer machine-guns us with information labeled in lettered zip codes of strategies to get us money. We might as well shoot ourselves now rather than go through the trouble of convincing the state to cough up. Thank God we don't need food stamps.

And my mother thinks that my brother is the only one in the family who needs help. "But you have Michael," she always tells me, like that explains why I don't get free vacations in Sicily like he does and the gift of a house from her, he's so "troubled." If she only knew what I was going through. It wouldn't make a bit of difference.

It's decided by a popular vote of disgust that we should go directly to the medical center that offers sliding scale operations. We are all relieved that microscopes won't be placed up our asses to determine just when and how we actually move our bowels.

This is no easy handout to get, Rush Limbaugh.

Earlier, a woman in the waiting room was trying to wheedle money out of the receptionist for her daughter's asthma medication. "She could die if she doesn't get it."

This makes me glad that I still have credit no matter how much it is currently maxed. Her desperation might even chill the cholesterol-clogged hearts of overindulged white men in Congress whose ideas of hardship range from having to drive their own cars instead of limos to working past 5PM one day a year. I can't believe that we pay that asshole in Utah, Orrin Hatch, to represent us in Congress. He firmly stated in public, "Women can't get pregnant when they are raped." Someone should rape him just for saying that.

I'm thinking of all the smugly rich people in the world who believe that they are more worthy than the people in this room waiting for help. The wealthy who feel guilty about their money because they aren't sharing any of it. I feel bad for these people who spend their days waiting on orange plastic chairs, wondering if they will get the cash advance or not.

Sitting there I felt more empathetic to people who run headlong into hard times and have nothing to show for it but bruises. I think of how divine it would be if every child born was wanted and not just tolerated. I am getting more and more steamed over the fact that a particular group of pigs wish to abolish welfare and food stamps and public assistance. After all, I myself am sitting here, requesting the largesse of the state to solve my husband's herniatic crisis. We had to pick this year to give up our health insurance. It doesn't matter, we would have coughed it up in Blue Shield payments already.

It's decided. We're not getting free money. We're having the operation in a hospital that will extend us interest-free revolving credit into the next millennium. Much better than being glued to orange plastic, waiting for our ship to come in bearing a check with our names on it.

Tax Day Looms

᷍ I was so worried I'd be hauled off to debtor's prison last week when I heard what I owed the IRS. It just so happens I have the money to pay them so I won't be handcuffed and thrown in the pokey for failure to comply with the law. Yippee!! This calls for a celebration. I think I'll go get compost on Sunday and redig the garden. I have simple needs. Okay, so I like cashmere too. And diamonds and sapphires but only if they're a gift.

It feels damn good to make some money and see my business skyrocket, so I can't complain too much that I owe those bomb-makers in Washington more pin money. Oh sure, they don't have to shoot the bombs off, they can just tell our eighteen-year-olds to do it for them. Eighteen is barely old enough to drive, for heaven's sake. If he got drafted we'd have to move to Canada and that would severely cut into his college tuition. You have to pay around $200,000 for the privilege of living in the Canadian Rockies. What's the world coming to?

Actually, all's right with the world 'cuz I can pay my taxes! What a statement. Next year I'm going plan ahead, even pay quarterly, so I don't get socked with this propane fury explosion in mid-April. I'm becoming a grown-up, I guess.

I have this face that suggests that all I do is drink Mai Tais and have the business acumen of Bill Murray. It isn't true. I do have worry lines about money but I'm doing yoga so they'll disappear. I'm always going be young no matter how old I get. It's an attitude thing. I love this feeling of not caring what people think so much. I'm still afflicted with it but it's getting better. Now that I'm almost forty-one I'm going to give it up altogether. Why be bothered about what someone else believes to be true about me? So fucking what? Trying to get approval is never, I repeat, NEVER any fun. And life is about sucking as much fun out of it as my pores can handle. That's why I have to stay open. God, I feel so ecstatic that we can pay taxes!

My esteem is higher because I'm shooting weddings by myself now. I don't have to share the earning capacity with Michael, who can now fend for himself and grow up into a man. And I work better expressing my own vision and not sharing the director's role. Okay, so filmmaking is a collabo-ration, but photography isn't and I get to do it my way. And be paid for that objective. That's why we made more money last year, because I started to realize that. Finally. I'm coming into my own now. Not hanging on the partnership of being considered Michael's sidekick when in fact it's my business.

I needed my own path in life and I have it now. We're all on this journey alone and we make the best of it as we travel along, bumping up against other people.

Just bungee jump right into my fear.

Everyday Epiphanies

Writing Muscles

௸ I have wanted to write since I was a child; when I locked my diary and hid the key, I got the most delicious feeling. I had expressed what I had wanted to say out loud but would be hit or ostracized if I did. In my diary I swore at my parents, bellowed at the nuns and said what I really thought about my friends and enemies. I knew that someday I would get away and have a real life where people might even listen to me and ask questions. Be concerned about the nature of my life and want to know the details.

So. Five years ago at the age of thirty-six, I said to myself I'm gonna let out everything inside of me and see what comes up the pipeline. I faced the page every day with my speedy pen and bled all over the whiteness and kept going until my hand hurt and my eyes started to blink shut. Some of it was tripe and some of it was God in the details like a shaft of light bayoneted through the loosely held boards of an old barn relaxing in the seasons and the wind. I kept on.

I didn't want to read it right away. It had to sit and incubate or fester or just stay in the darkness

until I had to read it and then, after it had been
some days since I wrote it, suddenly the thing
would mean something other than how I had written it. On good days it wrote itself, on other days I
was stretching.

Some people ask me rather derisively, "So what
do you write in those notebooks?" They "don't
have time to write" like I do but they always fan-
cied that someday they would write a book and
what makes me think that I can write a book?

I don't listen anymore and I don't tell people
that want to be envious or judgmental or just plain
mental about what I do when I'm alone in the
house every day, pouring my heart out onto my
sleeve, skipping stones on my soul. Why, that's
easy to do. If only they had the time in between
school and brain surgery and selling real estate,
which really makes a lot of money, did you know
that?

So I figured some things out in the last five
years. I like laughing an awful lot. I'd rather be
doing that than just about anything, even eating,
and I think that's why I've lost weight recently. I'm
busy following my curiosities like a volcano spew-
ing lava down its embankments. I've got to do this
now because I've been in my forties for a whole
year and I'm just figuring out that this is the best

decade of my life so far because I'm not embarrassed to be me, loud mouth and all. That's what
my father called me, "Big Mouth." I guess it stuck.

Writing is what I do every day, like walking and
reminding my kid to brush his teeth and smiling
and petting my dog and kissing my guy who has
been around for eighteen years. It just is. And ever
since I've started I've become a little bit saner and
speak with more clarity. Or is that because I gave
up pot?

I forget what I write and then when I read it a
few weeks later I see it in a new shaft of light, or I
decide that I was practicing that day and it needs
work. My older writing is more appealing now than
before because I have changed in the last few years
and the syntax shows that.

Julie told me today, "You've really done a lot of
new things this year," and that's when I told her
about my Maui trip, I'm taking all by myself. My
first retreat since being married and the only one
of my lifetime so far, in front of an ocean view in
the middle of the Pacific on volcanic rock. I am so
jazzed that I'm keeping this secret mostly to
myself. It's so delicious that I am guarding it like a
tender puppy that can't be let out to play in the
street. I want to avoid having my enthusiasm run
over by a fleet of Mack trucks.

It was the writing that did it for me. And also the therapy and Michael pushing me over that bottle of champagne. He was right. I am going and I'm so excited. I am in awe that I can be that good to myself. I'm going for the gusto in life and I'm not stopping just because it's expected that I'll feed the dog and keep gas in the car and remind Wolfe to finish his homework. I can shed my usual roles of caretaker and cash provider and go for the glory in Maui where I will relax and work hard, hobnobbing with the rich and powerful, aspiring and emerging. My path has lead me here and I'm following.

This is big, very big, and I'm doing it. When I think of it I get a lilt in my step and a jolt in my soul.

Onward into my fear and out the other side!

Melting Midriff Fat

⌒ I could no longer wedge hunks of blubber off my back with my bare hands. The fat just wasn't there anymore. What gives?

I decided to weigh myself.

This is a behavior I haven't indulged in since being double-dared to have my weight guessed at Great America a few years ago.

I stepped on the scale. It's probably just a few pounds.

Oh my God! Fifteen pounds had vanished!

Oh yeah, I had been sick and everything I ate was expelled from one orifice or another. I was looking svelte. I had also given up swimming. I was fitting in my skinny clothes now?!

I thought it was just because Michael got a day job outside the house and I no longer made lasagna for breakfast, lunch and dinner. But no, it was something else.

I was too busy juggling bowling balls to eat anymore! This is a major consciousness shift. I used to go see what was happening in the refrigerator at least every two hours. Now I was living my hours outside of the kitchen, cementing my focus on writing, photography work, taking the dog for a walk or scratching my fingers in the dirt to aerate my petunias. The refrigerator was losing its charm, its very hold on my life. But I hadn't noticed until my underwear started fitting again.

I was stupefied and delighted and ecstatic. I did not try to lose weight; it just happened. Me, who took four years to go back to exercise after spurting out a fully formed human being. Me, who arrived at a yoga class seven months pregnant and enjoyed the prostrate meditation at the end of the class better than the poses. Me, who swore off exercise for good when I realized that breastfeeding was a full-time job. Me, who wore sweatpants for ten years and am now tucking my shirts into my jeans for the first time in a decade. Tucking in? Did you hear me? I have a waist now!

People are noticing my melted fat now that it's summer and I'm not living in sweaters. A few people are happy for me. Most people suspiciously say, "You've lost weight," like I hacked it off with a saw from Jenny Craig or Richard Simmons. They particularly don't want to hear my effortless, vanishing fat story. And I just want to tell them, hey, do what you love to do and the fat goes away. It worked for me.

Simone, my eternal friend, who gets paid to be psychic, said to me once, "When it's time for the

fat to go it will go without effort." I thought, oh
sure, she's obviously on some fifth dimension right
now. But she was right. And I did it without those
high-priced boxes of frozen food or confessional
meetings.

I like to say it's all because of Michael getting a
real job, but then people want to talk about what he
does for a living and I was about to launch into my
revelations on fat transference.

It's weird. After I had diarrhea for two weeks,
food stopped looking so great. I had to be careful
about what I ate. It was just gonna get blown out
anyway. So why not stop eating and focus on a project instead? This is a revelation that took me forty
years to figure out. Instead of creating minimaster-
pieces of gourmet perfection and eating while
standing up without a napkin, I write some more,
do photography, hang with Wolfe.

In fact I'm giving up cooking and relying on
others to fill in the blank. Like Stouffer's and my
very own progeny. Why do I have to supply a bal-
anced meal of three major food groups for the family that lives here? Was I genetically programmed
for this behavior? Do I have an extra chromosome
for whipping up dinner every night?

It's finally occurred to me. I have other things to
do besides making bread and delivering meals to

the TV so *The Simpsons* won't be interrupted. I am giving up the antiquated notion of a New England dinnertime where we all eat boiled potatoes and politely inquire after the events of everyone's day. We can do that on the weekend. With a glass of wine to help it all go down. Now we just fight about where dinner will be served, who will make it, what we'll have with all the differing diets in the house and by then I'm ready to just give up eating entirely. I am going to carefully conceal the fact that I worked as a cook in restaurants for four years. Just because I have on-the-job training is no reason to mistake me for Julia Child. She gets paid to cook. I have talents that I don't have to use.

Eating is overrated anyway. I mean, I love to eat too much, but I just end up getting sick and feeling depraved that a whole bag of chips was consumed and it was my mouth that did the vacuuming. And besides I like to talk even more than I like to eat.

I just got back from lunch with Julie and after comparing her to a pastrami sandwich on rye, I forget about the sandwich and focus on her. It's hard to eat when I'm looking at her because my jaw drops open from her beauty and wit and insight and the BURGER ON MY PLATE DOESN'T LOOK AS GOOD. This is why I fit in size 10 pants now.

A milestone yesterday. A salesclerk said to me, "What size are you, 6 or 8?" I had to be scraped off the floor. No! Size 12. I told her. But the size 10 was nice and roomy, so I bought it. My first Armani pants, for the price of a small third-world country.

Julie pointed out to me today that when I had diarrhea I was stressed to the max. I hadn't thought of that. I was all worried about my marriage and Wolfe's college education and our home-life and everything else.

I'm glad my hair didn't start falling out in patches, because I just had it highlighted. But if it did I would just go bald and emulate the Zen priest look. So what?

So hey, all it took was considering a nervous breakdown. And you can do it too if you want.

I will try to maintain my balance even though life can be a choke hold in one of those dog collars that have pointed barbs all the way around it. I will try to avoid having a nervous breakdown unless it can be conveniently scheduled.

A Naked Soul and Jiggly Boobs

❧ Big realization today. When I racewalk, I actually feel more comfortable wearing a bra. This way I don't have to clutch my breasts as I speed by seventy-year-old men futzing in their gardens, and they don't have a heart attack from seeing my forty-year-old boobs bounce up and down. Jiggling and shaking as I sweat down the street is not much fun when I have an audience of retired men watching me from behind their picket-fence marriages. And wearing a bra keeps me from dripping sweat into my waistband.

Held in place like that, they actually look quite fetching. Maybe it's the gravity of being forty. All of a sudden I want to shave my legs, be a bottle blonde and quit jiggling so much when I walk.

It has to do with taking stock of my life. And looking forward to meditation more than a big bowl of chips laden with sour cream dip. This took decades to figure out.

An old man with his cane walks by me on the sidewalk as I throw out my hips and swing my arms ballasted by one-pound handweights. I feel like the Titanic before it hit the iceberg. He cheerily calls out to me, "It's exercise time!" I yell back to him through the morning air, "It feels good!" and keep striding.

Yes. It feels good to move my mass of muscle and jiggly fat and bone-deep neuroses that need some air. See, the whole benefit of motion is not just slimming down. It's the emotional charge of fresh wind blowing through my stuck attitudes that keeps me doing it. And the added bonus of more energy infused into my day overpowering my lard-ass tendencies. When I don't do it I just want to drink wine like a bohemian beatnik and pretend that I have a secretary who will arrive soon to write down my latest thoughts. I feel like having a bath, reading all day, maybe fingering a few glitzy clothes catalogs, topped off by dinner and a movie so I can say that I'm researching my next screen-play.

I get lazy.

But getting my blood moving in my veins is a high. I just didn't know that when I used to think of exercise as some grossly overrated mindless hour-eater. That was when I wore sweatpants big enough for three people, and happily surrendered to split ends and stretched-out T-shirts that someone else had already sweat in, and avoided getting off my duff ever.

But this bra thing is a revelation. The underwire boots my attitude. I feel womanly and firm and held in place by what I so recently thought was the rigid norms of a puritan society. Hey, maybe I just need to be professionally fitted for a bra so that I'll have one that I can wear without serrating my skin under my clothes.

The thing is I like my nipples brushing against my linen shirts and being allowed to breathe rather than reigned in by conventional thought and polyester.

But these D-cups shake so when I'm just minding my own business, picking out a watermelon at the grocery store, I feel the eyes of a usually much older man staring below my neckline straight into the aureoles under my shirt.

It's a naked feeling. I've been living with it for years, didn't think much of it until today, when my breasts looked so perky and rounded in a real bra.

My friend April would call this a midlife crisis.

I mean, I can take the innocent issue of a bra and turn it into a major revelation. I've lived forty years just to come to this conclusion: Bras do help.

Is it because my bustline is moving south?

The better I feel about myself, the more I want

to look good. Last week I was so excited about going camping that I put mascara on just to sleep outside in a tent at the ocean. I can't remember the last time I looked down a mascara wand.

But I'm starting to see that I've got some raw material to work with here—me. And instead of wearing my breasts around my waistband and blaspheming bras as torture devices invented by men, I'm going to march down to my neighborhood lingerie confections store and join the hordes of women who refuse to swing sweaty boobs from their chests. I'm older and wiser now and more conscious of the two years of breastfeeding that pulled my nipples out of their moorings. And I loved it too because that's what breasts are for! Not for jazzing up beer commercials or selling cars!

Another revelation. At the last wedding I shot, the bride, her sister, two pals and I escaped the crushing crowd in a fit of girlish fun to the bowels of the country club to bask in the glow of the bride's first married cigarette. Her sister, a Princeton grad with an English degree, had helped the bride gussy up her toast to the parents which made me cry.

"You're a writer!" I told her. Excited that here was a kindred spirit. She proceeded to tell me, "I'm not writing now. When I have kids and I'm at home I'll write. It's not very feasible to be a writer."

Gee. Her parents paid for that pricey degree from an Ivy League college and this is the outcome? I was stunned. Here she is young, beautiful, talented, with a firm bosom, and she's putting off writing until she can't do it when the babies come. I wanted to shake her! No! Don't do what I did. Let yourself go wild in your writing now while you don't have to wake up twelve times a night. Don't think you'll have more time later! When you haven't slept in years and a shower sounds like a trip to Europe. Her gorgeous face was grim in the light of the lone cigarette.

I wanted to say, you'll kick yourself for not starting sooner, forgetting moments that could have been committed to paper in the haze of being a fresh twenty-two-year-old ready for new adventures.

I knew she wouldn't listen so I kept my mouth shut. A habit I don't often indulge in.

But it emboldened me. I thought, here I am, a forty-year-old with saggy boobs who believes in myself enough to know that being a writer means writing every day and nurturing the delicious hope that, with perseverance and patience, my book will get published and then my screenplay will sell but even if it didn't I'd still write. I haven't given up like this beautiful and smart girl has by telling herself, "It isn't feasible to be a writer." Is that what Princeton did for her, help her to believe that she doesn't have a hope in hell of doing what she loves to do and is good at too?

It opened my eyes. People say, "I want to be a writer, painter, doctor, CEO, a licensed contractor." But then they don't do the motion that goes with it. Wanting and wishing is imagination fueling the soul. Then the muscles and brain take over. Do the thing that you must do, that you would do even without payment.

Hey, it might take years but the person who says, "I'm too old to learn piano," is going to be that age anyway without benefit of learning how to play a beloved instrument. And if we don't keep learning new things, we might as well be dead.

That's how I'm keeping a sparkle in my chassis. By being curious and not saving my passion for another time in the future when things will be different.

I've been writing for five years and I feel like I'm just beginning to crack the nut meat inside me. To get to the core of what ails me, the center of what elates me and the power of creating every day.

I'm breaking the surface of the water now like a diver in the Olympics on the high platform. I jumped off and now, after falling through the air for five years, I'm just beginning to touch the water

and discover this profound world beneath the surface. I saw the water but I didn't know what was
there until I stepped off what passes for terra firma
and took the free fall down into the depths of my
own soul.

There's a whole world in here. A world that
whispers my truth to me and feeds me fortitude
when the world outside gives me half-truths and
slander.

It's a place where I talk to God and hear the
word "yes," not "it isn't feasible." A place that is
right here, no plane rides; it's under my skin. Just
under the surface of the water.

A world that sustains me. Ripe with miracles
and joy. Under the facade of perky boobs in a bra
beats the soul of a woman diving into the chasm of
curiosity without hard facts on what's at the bottom of the pool.

I'm jumping anyway. There isn't any other time
to do it. Only now.

Foundation Finery

༒ I showered this morning and then decided, to hell with it, I'm not saving my new lingerie for a special occasion! I'm going to feel important right now! And all it takes is a new underwire bra and matching panties to send me soaring.

I walked Fluffy down to the local *haute* lingerie store opened by a gorgeous woman from Berlin, Gitti. She knows exactly what you're looking for even when you don't. She has crackly blue eyes that spark mischief and all-nighters of romance. This is where to go when I need a visit with a wise woman. Fluffy, being a French poodle, was welcomed with open arms. I knew he wouldn't lift his leg on any of the silken creations from Italy, hanging like lacy handkerchiefs from padded hangers, lining the walls staring at me with bows between their cups.

I was agog. Fascinated by all the finery, sucked in by the spectacular cleavages with no one in them. Bras from only the most sensuous countries: France, Italy, Austria, Switzerland, Ireland. My head was swirling with the romantic possibilities, when I would rip off my outerwear or be plucked out of it to reveal my new layer of silken luxury lying next to my most intimate parts.

But my arm was being pulled out of its socket by a well-brushed dog leading me sharply to every corner of the couture-laden store. I wanted to finger lace-edged camisoles from Ireland and Fluffy wanted to stick his snout in the matching panties hanging lower at floor level.

I was drawn to the bras featured near the front door in a most tantalizing way. They looked so creamy and able to be worn by a woman who might be climbing over a fence or rolling across wet grass in a soccer game. The bow between the cups was not as pronounced as some of the others.

"This is the new fabric, microfiber—it's supposed to breathe just like cotton!" the salesclerk said brightly.

"Does it?" I questioned darkly.

"I tried it on yesterday and it felt good. It's the underwire that you might have to get used to."

I'm just not a bra kind of person. Bras are for sex. They are supposed to be salivated over and then removed by your lover's teeth.

But the other day at April's shower I bent down in my linen tank top revealing my entire décolletage and everything south of the equator. I suddenly felt that hanging 38Ds were a view I didn't

mind ten women staring at but felt that the tele-
phone repairman across the street, Wolfe's male
teacher and retired men in their gardens at 10AM
didn't need to know about them. Quite frankly, I've
been flashing for several years now, decades even,
and never gave it a thought. Now I'm forty and
tired of having my boobs talked to and not me. But,
ironically, I've been against bras ever since I was
big enough to fit in one.

When I was eleven, flat as a front door and desperate for a training bra, it meant the height of
womanly allure and attainment. It meant maturity,
having a period, someday having a baby! It was
about giving up undershirts and becoming a real
woman.

So I thought I'd give this microfiber a whirl. The
salesclerk assured me, "It's the most reasonably
priced bra in the store." I thought the price tag said
$62 but it was really $29. I could even afford to
buy it. For uplifted boobs, why not? I took Fluffy
into the dressing room and stood on his leash so he
wouldn't bolt. After a while I figured I was spending money here so I let him slip under the curtain
to wander freely among the silk teddies. Oh my!
The bra fit and it looked good too. And matching
panties too? I was in heaven! This was a bold move,
a decision to rein in my breasts, to reduce their

floppy gait as they swing down the street indepen-
dently of me.

And now as I sit here, building up my tolerance
to an underwire like breaking in new boots, I feel
this soft secret under my Levi's shorts. It feels like
underneath my mainstream mother facade lies the
heart of a passionate woman, simmering under the
surface of my suburban duties, being a breadwin-
ner, a limo driver, a woman who insists homework
be finished before dark. I didn't realize foundation
garments would do this for me. Under my clothes,
a sultry seductress lurks, as apt to schedule a weekend away with loverman as I am to engage in a hot
fudge sundae with Wolfe without even a fleeting
thought of calories.

And here I was avoiding man-made fiber all
these years.

In my new panties I can do anything!

Sex After Death

∾ I drove our thirty-year-old car, which sometimes has to be started with a screwdriver, to San Francisco for a seminar and returned late at night to hear Michael say, "I was worried about you. I thought you got in an accident and were lying dead on the road. (Pause) Then I started thinking I could be with your sister 'cuz she has your essence, so it would be sort of like being with you."

I've been gone for eight hours and my husband has already married my sister, deciding it's the closest thing to being with me. But then I show up and he's relieved that he doesn't have to go through the courting process with her.

So. If the spouse dies tomorrow who would you be with?

Last night we had a round table discussion with two old friends married to each other. Heavily watered with scotch we weren't shy about our answers. Diana says, "Leif, if you touch my sister after I'm dead I'll kill you. You wouldn't, would you?"

"I don't know, maybe," he says. That wasn't the right answer.

She puts her arm around me, saying, "You can't

just boink your wife's sister or your husband's brother. Take Deborah instead—she'd be good for you but not my sister!" (Deborah's her best friend.)

Leif says, "I like your sister better."

"I can't believe you guys, wanting to be with our own flesh-and-blood sisters. As if we're alike in some way. I wouldn't touch one of your brothers."

"That's because you already got the best one, so why bother?" I've met each one of Leif's brothers and he's definitely the pick of the litter.

"How could you even think about who you'd be with when none of us are dead yet?" Diana says.

I tell them, "Don't you guys talk like this? We do this on dates. And besides, haven't you seen *Legends of the Fall?* I know who I'd be with." They all look at me. Except Michael who already knows.

"Come on, tell us."

"No way, I'm not saying."

They can wait and find out if it happens. It's certainly thought-provoking to wonder who the lover/spouse/partner will end up with when you're out of sight. The thing is we go on being attracted to other people. Sometimes I wonder how my life might be if I suddenly had to deal with Michael being gone. I don't think this has anything to do with the fact that I want him to get a real job to pay back all his bills.

It does make me appreciate him more. People get hit by cars, get sick, change drastically. We just don't know all the time how secure our little lives are. Sure, I tell myself we'll be together on our front-porch rocking chairs, laughing hysterically and still enjoying every minute. But there are no guarantees. People up and die on you.

Then sisters and brothers come to console the remaining spouse and suddenly you find new arms around you. Life keeps happening and you aren't dead yet, so why not wake up and live? This could happen to a woman whose dead husband's brother comes to comfort her.

It was all explained visually in *Legends of the Fall*. The three brothers go off to war. Julia Ormond stays home to wait for the youngest one to return so they can get married. He gets shot and his two brothers come home with his heart in a box for their father, who learned about some Indian ritual that says you have to do that when someone dies. Both brothers fall in love with her. The grieving beautiful left-behind babe. Smart too. The wild brother gets her after some great fun in a hot tub. Who wouldn't want to be in hot water with Brad Pitt? Then he leaves her to "find himself," traveling the sea and madly fucking in soft-focus orgies. She pines away for him for two years, then he writes her a cryptic note, "Don't wait for me, I'm no good for you." Big crescendo of music, tears, pain and suffering. Then the conservative, no-fun brother shows up to comfort her and convinces her to marry him.

Julia gets the big house, fancy clothes, servants and—big surprise—she's still bored. She wants adventure and orgasms and starry-eyed enchantment, not straight laced politicking cocktail parties to vote her husband into Congress. It's boring and she liked the brother with the long hair, sleek muscley body and amazingly luscious lips. Brad Pitt. He has a way of smiling and riding a horse at the same time that opens your eyes a couple notches and makes you all shivery. Of course she still wants him. It doesn't matter that his younger brother was her first lay and his older brother is now her husband.

It just goes to show that fun rules. Sexiness, high spirits and prolonged interested staring are a lot better than IRAs, mediocre sex and dinner every night at exactly 6PM.

Okay, so I ruined the movie for you. But see it anyway just for the way Brad looks at Julia and how she looks back. It's how all love affairs should start.

So who's to say if your lover wouldn't be happy with your sister after you die? Diana says, "My sister is so different from me. She's younger and prettier. It wouldn't be like having my essence at all."

"You don't really agree with her, do you?" Michael asks when Diana goes out to the front porch for a cigarette after all this pontificating on sex with family members—pardon me, in-laws.

"Yeah, being a human living on this earth I do, but when I'm dead I'll be with people I want to be with. I'll be happy where I'm going, so how could I hate you for sleeping with my sister from that place?"

Once you're dead you get booted up to a higher level, more wattage, more gigabytes and more RAM. You don't bum out on how it used to be before you got off the train. You just are. You're not obsessed with getting back at your lover for marrying your sister. You're having too much fun yourself to care. It only sounds bad being on earth now and imagining them together, flagrantly fucking their brains out right in front of you. But it's not like that.

For one thing it has to be a lot easier to be dead than alive and watching your lover divorce you and take up with some other cute babe right in the same town. Being dead isn't hanging around here all the time, watching our antics. Dead people have better things to do. Just read *Embraced by the Light* if you don't believe me.

This life stuff is just a testing ground, an experiment in divinity, a practice race, around-the-lap-pool kind of deal. Along the way we learn stuff and then we die and we're on a new plane of existence learning more high-voltage stuff.

It's hard to imagine our husbands banging our sisters. But from another dimension in time we simply wouldn't get worked up about it.

I'm planning on having a great time in the next life. It will be like walking though a door to another room. And if it isn't like that I'll be surprised and find out how to be in a world I have never experienced before.

While I was reading *Embraced by the Light* I just kept nodding my head up and down. It all fit for me. The panels of angels, the dark tunnel leading to brilliant light, the relatives back on earth calling my name because of course they don't want me to go. It all sounds too good to whine about how my husband, who I left behind holding all the dirty laundry, is boinking my sister. So what? When you hang around with angels flying through dimensions to other time zones and meeting all the people you used to know before they died, who has time to worry about the people you loved in the last lifetime? From that place I'm just gonna be happy they're getting their rocks off. Yes, this is an oblique way of saying it's okay to end up with my sister after I'm dead, but if you try it before I'll kill you.

Michael and I talked about replacement lovers over coffee the next morning. Wolfe hears us and knows immediately who I'd marry. God, I'm so transparent even my kid knows without me saying anything. It's nobody you know. Just a well-built guy with a flashing grin, razor-sharp humor and a challenging mind. Like the one I have now.

What I love about Michael I would carry over into the next love affair, looking for similar kinds of attributes if he kicks. He immediately thought of my sister when he imagined me lying dead in a ditch. Of course I think my sister is nothing like me. But she is beautiful, smart and funny and I've heard she's a good lay, so why not? I mean I've already got someone lined up so why shouldn't he?

This makes me wonder about the fascinating aspects of being married to one person for decades. We have this rock-solid commitment between us and the longer it gets the more we realize how rare it is. Being an adventurous spirit I wonder and feel blessed at the same time about the longevity of it. The crap that can happen, disease, accidents, whatever. It makes me see the fragility of life. Like a flower blooming and then decaying because it was hit by a kid's Frisbee or died from natural causes.

Life is like that.

I get so hypnotized by the belief that things last forever. They don't. Nothing does and that's what makes it all blossom with rainbows, deep eloquent sighs and gargantuan sideboards of lobster and crab.

Every moment is rich in possibility when I truly realize that it could be my last here.

Money, Heat and Marriage

ॐ Oh my God! I'm recovering from the biggest wedding I've ever photographed alone. This was complemented by 100-degree weather, bathing me in sweat from my waist to my armpits. I figured the bride and groom wouldn't notice; they only had eyes for each other.

They were so young that they looked good standing in the full glare of the harsh sun. They weren't even out of college yet! Their parents were my age, which is really scary. They thought it was fine for them to get married. The bride couldn't be pregnant because they were Born Agains and everyone knows that Christians only have sex to procreate, not to have fun. When I laid eyes on the groom for the first time I thought I needed a double. I thought, aren't you too young to get married since you're not old enough to vote?

But I'm proud of myself for shooting it alone with two videographers who both wanted my sight line. I nearly lost it when, wanting to be conservative, I took far fewer pictures than I usually do so that the bride and groom would not wilt in the beating heat. Meantime, the video gal makes them fool around for her camera, playing peekaboo with the trees and winking at each other fakely, topped off by spinning around in a circle holding hands. I swallowed my outrage, which always gives me a headache.

We finally got to the twelve-acre estate in Carmel with the pool and tennis court and landscaped gardens and half-mile driveway lined with maple trees. Then I discovered there was no booze. What a letdown. Oh well. My head felt like you could fry eggs on it so I accepted some fake champagne and just shut up. Michael was not there to complain to.

It was fun to tell the groom's father that the pictures were not done when he wanted them to be. He's used to getting his way. He's the CEO of a company so huge I can't even tell you what it is because I don't want to spend all of next year in court for libel.

I liked his wife. She raised four boys who still love her.

When the groom was being whisked away with his bride in the 1966 Mustang, which still looks like a new car to me, his last words were, "Where's my mom?" The newlyweds remained rooted to the blacktop until Mom arrived to kiss her son good-bye. That moved me to tears. And also when the bride was coming down the aisle wrapped in a fairy-tale dress that looked like the good witch Glinda in *The Wizard of Oz.* That was the first time I laid eyes on her, walking backwards and holding a Hasselblad to my face, shouting pleasantries over the string quartet. "Nice to meet you," she says as her parents, who are my age, escort this fragile fawn toward the very grown-up institution of Marriage.

Heady brew. Then, since they were young, the bride and groom stood in the blaring sun and recited their vows. The parents' friends looked on and then dashed out of the heat and onto cable cars, which took them to their boozeless reception.

I was having fun until two people stood up and sang a song about how we all have to clean up our souls "and take the trash out." I wanted to throw tomatoes at them but everyone else was politely stifling yawns so I refrained. Then they launched into another song and that's when I had to be nailed down. Must we be reminded of religion right now? Can't we just dance and talk and laugh without thinking about Jesus? That was the boring part. I guess they figured they had 200 captive people so why not teach them a thing or two about God? Geez!

When the bride changed I was thinking, I'm seeing her naked before the groom does. They were too holy to have premarital sex. She didn't look old enough. She toasted him by saying, "We'll have lots of babies." The thought of unbridled sex sent everyone into a swoon, especially the Christians.

The bride and groom were so handsome they even looked good being tired. I looked like someone had driven a tractor over me.

I feel older and wiser today.

I am now old enough to have had a child get married if I had forgotten to take my birth control pills twenty years ago. But twenty-year-olds are not old enough to have babies. The bride looked so young and fresh, not old and grizzled like me. And I like my grizzledom. The less I defend my viewpoint the better. I am finding that just being myself is a lot more fun than being who I think people want me to be.

After the bride and groom shoved off I took a few time-exposed pictures and then thought, I'll say good-bye to the groom's parents, and then I'm telling myself, they don't want to be interrupted so I'll just slink off.

I realized what a wimp I was being, so I walked up to their intimate party table in the dark by the

pool and sat down to say good-bye to the mother
who raised four sons who still love her and hold
her hands and look in her eyes. And she glowed
and we both felt close for a moment and I was glad
I didn't let their wealth intimidate me. I wanted to
thank them for being who they are, for having me
photograph their first son's wedding.

I felt complete as I drove off in my air-conditioned car that was waiting at the curb for me,
delivered by the valet service.

And I did it all myself. I have a larger dose of
confidence today. Incrementally widening my band
of spiritual acknowledgment of my own gifts. They
paid me to be there without meeting me first. They
trusted me before meeting me to do a great job for
them. Maybe these Born Agains have the right idea
after all. Their faith can and does move mountains.
What's a little lack of booze when your son still
wants to kiss you in front of 200 people? They
must be doing something right.

Maybe I should take some lessons from them.
I'll just leave in the cocktails.

I like peeking into other people's lives and
observing them within the intimacy of a wedding.
Watching them tick slowly in front of me, I get to
take pictures while they forget I'm there. It was a
different world than the one I inhabit. A world

where the children have their own wing of the house away from the parents.

And their own white stone lions guarding the front door. And a housekeeper who irons and puts out cold drinks for them without being asked. And their own cook who serves all their meals in the formal dining room.

Does wealth make us different or are we different before the wealth is accrued? There is something spiritually enticing about figuring that out. I think the only difference between them and me is that they believe in themselves more. They have accepted good fortune while I live in disbelief that I'll ever have my own pool and exotic flower arrangements, flown in from Hawaii, gracing the tables at my latest party, and vacations whenever I want them. In my heart I find this hard to believe.

Someday I'll snap out of this and then I'll drive a car from this century. A new car manufactured so recently that it still smells new. Without crumbling upholstery.

Someday when I figure out I'm a queen and not a spiritual pauper. Someday, maybe this week even.

Getting to God without Scotch

I Ran Away to Maui

❧ I was ready to put my head in the oven and get it over with. But Wolfe was heating up frozen fettucini, so instead I ran away from home and came back a changed woman.

Whenever the thought of annihilation enters the mind, it's far better to kiss the dog and the rest of the family good-bye and set out to parts unknown. With a plane ticket in hand. Somewhere you've never been before so you don't have to remember being there with someone else.

I got on the plane and noticed something was different right away.

I was reading a magazine and no one was asking me when the peanuts and Cokes would be served.

And I didn't have my purse with me!

I bolted out of my seat, instantly sweaty, and pole-vaulted over babies and mothers and women reading adult novels. I thought it was in the bathroom hanging on a hook but the attendants insisted I was mistaken. I yelled into the air space over the toilet cubicles, "I left my purse here but I don't remember which stall!"

A woman about to pee raised her eyebrows with disdain dripping and said, "You don't remember which stall you were in?" Like I was some sort of drug addict. Sorry, but I gave up coke years ago.

I had a plane to Nirvana waiting for me and I'm missing my wallet. The new wallet that got lost in the UPS strike. With 200 bucks in it. I was a mess. A crumpled, semihysterical, near-prostrate mess in search of a sedative. My mind went south all the way to a rubber room without a straitjacket. Ran in my new Nikes to the security gate, thinking, how can they help? Suddenly. A dim light went on in my sober mind. I never picked up my fanny pack from the X-ray table! In the haze of running away from home I had shorted out and left my personal effects behind. Why did I need baggage when I was going to float above the ground for ten days?

The security guard produced my fanny pack from her office. It was tagged like the toe of a corpse in a morgue. This solid-gold platinum gem of a woman, my angel, amazed me. I squeezed her for all she was worth. I ran back to the plane just before they closed the doors after the cardboard entrées had been rolled inside. Suffering over.

The five-hour ride went like thirty minutes.

I touched down in paradise and was hit with a

wave of balmy frangipani and rustling palm fronds
like an intoxicating ether bathing my soul. I never
wanted to leave!

An ocean-view room just for me! Hey. This is
what Francis Ford Coppola does. He stays in fancy
hotels and writes. There are a lot stupider ways to
spend a pile of cash when all is said and done. In
air-conditioned comfort and marble I can soar!

Tomorrow is the first day of my Screenwriters
Retreat. I decided to go all the way. I signed up for
the Siddha Rejuvenation Treatment for aristocracy
and Indian royalty. One must be ready to meet the
bigwigs.

I keep reminding myself that I'm here to work.
You know, to meet Ron Howard.

I was exiting my Siddha Rejuvenation Treatment when I ran smack-dab into him at the squash
court. Ron fuckin' Howard! I was so relaxed from
my hot oil that I started in on him, shaking his
hand and not even spasming my own muscles in
an attempt to calm down and breathe naturally. I
was not a jangled mess of celebrity idolatry in
search of a shred of self-esteem. Ron Howard was
on vacation just like me. In fact he's human in the
same way that I am. He's a parent, a communica-
tor and person who has to eject bodily wastes just
like all of us do. I walked away from him realizing,

I shook his hand and I wasn't paralyzed with fear!
What a revelation!

Soon I was walking up to best-selling authors,
acting like they should talk to me. And they did.
They gave me more attention than the mothers I
know here who interrupt everything I say with
some insightful comment about how they need a
spreadsheet to coordinate the schedules of three
kids for soccer. Or how they had a really difficult
time waking up this weekend because the kids
were at their ex-husband's house and they didn't
have to do anything. Moan and groan.

I got to talk with Ron four or five more times
after that. And he always answered my questions
about filmmaking and listened to me speak
without butting in. Okay, so I didn't get his
personal phone number but I know a lot of people
whose phone numbers I wish I could forget.

And another thing. I got to be with real writers.
To make friends with people who know what it
means to labor under the assumption that we have
something worthwhile to say, even though the kids
are asking for dinner and friends are wondering if
you've lost your mind because where is your writing going? Will it ever get published?

When I told my mother about being accepted
into the screenwriting program, she said, "I can't

believe you're so talented." None of my new friends would say that. Instead, Angie was handing me a pad of paper and a pen saying, "Write down what you just said!"

I don't get that at home. My kid says, "Were you talking to me?" after I've delivered a sermon on why he should practice his trumpet and Michael can't remember that we agreed on no TV for Wolfe before school. It was nice to be listened to for a change. Even if those high-powered, high-testosterone Hollywood agents didn't get my screenplay at all. So what?

Here's what I learned. It's a lot more fun to hang out with people who are actively taking a chance to fall on their faces, just like I did when my pitch to those agents bombed after my mouth dried up. I was scared to death to get up in front of the class and discuss my screenplay on an overhead, but I had to do it. After the first couple of minutes I stopped shaking and started to breathe again. Especially when the floor was being taken from me by a fellow student who had modeled nude before and was regaling the class with his exploits. I wanted the attention back on me right quick.

So I got over it. Shaking and quaking with fear is good. As long as it doesn't result in paralysis of the nervous system and you never do anything unfamiliar again. I had to pretend I was confident even though I felt like being transported on a gurney to a rubber room. Then when I met Veronica, the editorial director of Celestial Arts, and she said, "I want this!" meaning my book, I was floored. I wanted to dance around the room and hug her. I think I did. But it wouldn't have happened if I had wimped out and didn't face it when God told me, "GO to Maui even though you don't know how to set the margins on your computer."

Pretty soon I was hugging everyone like I normally do at home. It just didn't seem to matter that they were hotshot agents and accomplished authors. They are just people after all and I have a lot in common with them. Mainly because they let me finish my sentences and were interested in what I had to say.

I have a renewed sense of my purpose in life and it isn't just to earn money to pay back bills and provide insightful commentary on other people's dreams. I'm risking this now more than ever because I just can't shut up anymore, waiting for others to fall into my suggestions on how they should be so I can be a successful author, merrily writing away in my bedroom with the door closed.

I had to go to Maui to learn that. I took myself

away on retreat and discovered who I am apart from all the demands and roles I play here at home. I found out that I have a soul quaking in my rafting shoes and I'm going to let it out, even when others wish I'd just shut up and listen to their harangue about their pointless lives. Why do people use me as an unpaid therapist? 'Cuz I'm such a good listener. Which means they want to talk and I can listen without comment.

I feel so much more whole now after that experience. Thicker hide in the rejection area. More impervious to the discouraging comments of loved ones who wish that I'd just heat them up a frozen box of ravioli and listen to their boyfriend woes.

This trip really smoothed out the wrinkles in my forehead and the furrows in my soul. I learned so much on this trip that when it was time to go home, I cried. I didn't want to leave Brenda, my soul-mate sister whom it took five seconds to fall in love with while we waited in line to register. She lights up my world with her wit and retinas that bathe me with her brilliance, and digs a foundation under my dreams while accepting me as I really am. We decided to run away together until it dawned us—our pets would miss us too much. I wanted to keep learning and not have to go back to reality where the dog needs walking and the hot dogs need burning and the bills need paying. I needed another week in my marble and granite aerie.

I can make people laugh and that is a high like sex on a cloudy day. Maybe even better.

Roller Coasters and God

~ I was hurtling through the billowy black of a tunnel on my way to the top of the biggest dip on the roller coaster, the Giant Dipper in Santa Cruz. I wanted to feel the stars against my bare hands so I had carried the tickets in my wallet all year, waiting and hoping to get in this seat, climbing halfway to the sky and then plummeting down the track, free-falling with glee and terror etched on my face.

I saw it in the video afterwards. The look on my face was between bliss and dying. That train was taking me to a new plateau, a new universe where I saw God.

Inspired by the youth in front of me, I held my arms in the air for the first time in my life for the whole ride and it felt fluid and relaxed. It's better than holding on. And I like to scream too.

As we climbed the first huge hill, the last car in the lineup of ten, the Maxfield Parrish sky opened up through the white wooden tracks and I let go of everything that had ever held me down. Now the kids in front of me were screaming too.

When we first got on the ride they said, "Can we have your seat?" They wanted the last car. After we told them no dice, they snidely said, "You don't have padding on the back of your seat—you'll get whiplash."

My answer was, "Don't you want to puke on this ride?"

"Puke is not a word in my vocabulary," this kid half my size said.

The biggest dip was right now as the first car up ahead plunged into the warm night on sheer energy, leaving all mediocrity and holding back behind. You just have to let go and let your soul soar. There's no other choice but to go along with the rest of the cars and be skyrocketed through space, looped around curves and thrown against the side of the car without padding when a hard curve meets *you* faster than the box you're riding in. Two minutes of sheer terror rolled into a bite-sized piece suitable for framing in a video grab.

I said, "Let's go again and sit in the front."

I was giddy to get in line and wait with others who wanted to leave the cares of the world behind for two brief moments, suspended between the hard surface of reality and the whoosh of a free fall in the sky. On that car life doesn't exist as we know it. God is taking us for a ride, throwing us

against the stars and we'll never be the same again.
And I have the multiple black-and-blues to prove it.

I'm going back there to see God again.

It was the end of a perfect date. Dinner at the
Shadowbrook, hiking at Loch Lomond and now
this. Seeing God in my heart as I drop from the
biggest dip this side of the Mississippi.

Spirit Over Icicles

꘎ There's nothing like a cold swim on a freezing morning in frigid water to wake up my mind all the way down to my toenails and up through every nerve ending I have, and some I didn't know about. Plants are frozen outside and I decide it's not too cold to go swimming. Yeah, and it's fine to have ice cubes for ears, nipples the size of meatballs and every inch of my skin puckered into gooseflesh, but no, I couldn't just take a brisk walk; I had to go swimming.

I figured it's good for my mind to walk across icy concrete and plunge into 72-degree water. It's just water. And it's warmer than the temperature of the air.

I'm still cold. But it sure woke me up.

I got to the pool, discovered that the heating system was out of whack and considered wimping out. After all, I could see my breath billowing in the air. So this is why people go to the YMCA, to swim in an indoor pool, protected from blustery winds as they walk dripping wet from the pool to the locker room. I pooh pooh-ed such overconcern for their inflated comfort levels.

I am a mountain woman who has ushered in twenty snowy subzero-windchill-factored winters in Upstate New York, which rivals any weather happening in Alaska. It's an Arctic Circle attitude that just hasn't left me in fifteen California winters. I don't even consider this Palo Alto morning a "winter" wake-up. It isn't anything close to a 5-degree walk in Syracuse to get to your frozen car that won't start without major resuscitation from AAA, a battery charger or a hot water bottle placed over the ignition.

I try to remember all this as I head towards the pool, a bit of Lycra and cotton on my torso shielding me from the 40-degree air. Well gee, the water is thirty-six degrees warmer than my protruding-into-space nipples feel right now. My feet begin to freeze, walking over the glacially cold pool deck. The water will be a relief after this homestretch.

It isn't. I put my frozen feet in the water and consider changing back into my clothes and going home. This is not a human level of comfortable exercise. I'll do a run, I'll go home and eat. Anything but cold water on a 40-degree morning in late January as I round the bend of my fourth decade on earth.

But no, this is making me younger, not older. There are other people in the pool swimming who have me eclipsed by twenty years. They didn't scream with pain after jumping in the water. They got in and started their crawl. And probably had their hair turn white too.

It's mind over matter. The more I thought about how awful it would be to my warm body, the quicker I negated my enjoyment of the swim. I was talking myself back into my car, resisting cold and telling myself, you can't do this—it's too much, too Antarctica, too beyond comfort.

I tried not to let my scared-stiff thoughts consume me in paralysis. I remembered jumping out of that plane twenty years ago. This wasn't as extreme as parachuting, skiing or motorcycling, it was just cold. I felt like one of those polar bear people who jump in frigid water during winter and get out smiling. Their faces beam gratitude for life and a warm winter coat.

So I jumped in and I felt victorious even though I could only stand it for twenty-five minutes. I began to imagine hot coffee and warm food being eaten inside a house far from frigid air. Indoors where normal people are right now.

If I can face cold water on a "winter" morning, I can face other discomforts, still be elegant and see more clearly. It's only when I abandon an over-concern with my own comfort that I learn anything. My eyes are more open after swimming in ice water. My skin has been shocked into coming alive, no longer acquiescing to stay-at-home-in-my-warm-cave consciousness, ignoring my mind's warning not to venture out into the cold raw reality of walking almost naked on a wintry morn to dive into barely heated water.

As I stroked up and down the pool I asked myself, so what am I afraid of? I'm willing to be cold; I give up my warm home on a gray morning, filled with stiffly frozen lawns and not an ounce of sunshine, to jump into the unknown of a cold water swim just to wake up and pump my muscles. But it wasn't just the physical that made me plunge.

It was the spiritual nudge rising up from my soul that forced me into that crushed ice, pushing me up a cliff I didn't want to climb. I thought of those people who climb Mt. Everest and are asked, "Why do you do it?" And they answer, "Because it's there."

I couldn't wimp out and go home; I would have felt small and insignificant and afraid. Instead I felt alive, independent, awake and as cold as a flash-frozen box of chicken thighs.

I walked toward the pool and brightened when I looked into the face of a sixtyish, white-haired, benippled smiling woman getting out of the pool after her swim. "You can do it," she told me. She sure wasn't dead yet. She looked more alive than most women I know twenty years her junior, more alive than I did gingerly dabbling my frozen hand in the pool water.

If she can do it, so can I. I'm not going to shrivel up and stop living until I'm dead, even if it kills me.

So I jumped in and I'm still shivering, but what the hell, every cell in my body is at attention, my soul unmoored from its sluggish morning out-post.

I'm alive!

Giving Up the Seventies

∾ I don't know about you but my mother-in-law will not baby-sit while I do mushrooms with her son. No more LSD because it would interfere with my kid's soccer games. I couldn't be laughing on windowpane and cheerleading on the sidelines and providing the team snack all at the same time. It was necessary to give up grass when my kid pointed out to us, "Why do you guys smoke that stuff in the basement? It's yucky."

He did have a point. Now we '70s kids have given up drugs in favor of therapy. The list gets longer every day. I tell insiders, "It took six months of therapy to establish my kid's bedtime and be firm about him finishing homework every night. Then I delightedly hear, "I'm in therapy, too." Thank God it isn't just me; everyone else is fucked up too.

Now that we've given up pot and maybe even booze, what do we have left? Our own souls staring at us, bellowing, "Listen to me!" That's what I hear now. I've dug down below that protective layer of fog I used to surround myself with. That soft downy cloud that appeared the minute I inhaled. A sheath to keep out reality. And through the mist I'm wondering, geez, will my kid inadvertently turn me into the authorities for doing this? After all, he has yearly classroom visits from cops who denounce drugs and all their multicolored glory.

We no longer have to travel with a bong anymore. Our luggage is lighter now that we don't purchase lids and quarter pounds are out of the question. Sinsemilla costs too much.

A friend we hadn't seen in years said, "Let's get together for a glass of wine."

I said, "More than that!"

He said, "Okay, some heroin."

No, we had to give that up.

Okay, I never tried heroin, but the point is we feed our babies in the middle of the night, show up for teacher conferences, finish work we've promised to clients on a deadline; there's no time to have a glass of wine anymore, let alone get stoned. I'm a weekend drinker now. I had to admit that homework was interfering with my cocktail hour. Another crutch ripped away!

It took family therapy and a willingness to believe that change is good, even if it hurts. But I do grow horns when I drink too much scotch. I am in training to allow myself a few social drinks, not the entire bottle. Last weekend I drank too much and I woke up wondering if I should do a 12-step program. I thought about throwing up but I realized that all it takes is not drinking.

I like myself more when I'm clear. All busy and organized and focused on being in the moment. Two glasses of champagne and I'm giddy but five glasses and I'm wondering who should drive me home. I tell myself that the taste of wine is so luscious but it's just masking my lush tendencies. I do drink for the high just like I did when I smoked grass.

I don't miss smoking anymore because now I can answer the phone. When I was stoned I knew answering the phone meant I'd say something too "oh wow" to a potential client, an in-law or a lawyer. Other people were out there being effective while I was sitting on my front porch hearing the oak trees talk to me. I still hear the sounds and spirit of trees but not through a smoky haze. The clarity is more subtle, less booming. More authentic. That's the big surprise about giving up grass. I thought the hard edges of life would be more defined, more cutting and jaggedly hurtful, but instead I see more clearly the soft sweetness of reality underneath the facades we show the world. Blustering ego doesn't hit me with an ax anymore.

I see the insecurity beneath it and feel unharmed. Deadening myself from the slings and arrows of truth worked for decades. Now that the haze has lifted, I see how fragile we all are more clearly. We hide our tenderness so as not to be hurt, but showing it would heal ourselves and the world. But it's easier to just drink too much chardonnay and too many martinis.

Drinking is the only thing we have left besides Prozac and lithium. We've had to give up buying ounces and Valium and become upstanding citizens who vote, drive carpools and rally for more stop signs in our neighborhoods. These activities do not go well with meandering through meadows, tripping on mushrooms. The baby needs changing, the credit card debt needs paying and we've had to grow up and be real rather than stay immature and be stoned all the time.

Being awake is the way out of the fog. It's better than being trashed because we can still drive a car, talk to the kid's teacher and make cold calls. There just isn't time anymore to loll around being ripped and watching ants crawl across concrete. I know there's a way to mix magic with reality without resorting to mushrooms.

I'm a parent now, not a drug-addicted artist. I have to be on time when I pick up my kid from silk painting class. I have to show up and possibly drive a motor vehicle to get there. I am a grown-up now. I even have life insurance.

God, do I need a weekend alone with loverman at a luxury hotel.

Falling in Love

᭰ She was standing on my porch as I threw open the front door and I instantly fell in love. My new best friend. She sparkled, smiled and laughed hard. We clicked immediately and I knew this is a friend I'll have forever.

Her mother had hired me months before to photograph her daughter's wedding, saying, "I know Jillian will like you!"

And there she was coming into my life and knocking my socks off.

We couldn't take our eyes off each other. My breath was beaten out of me by this dreamy rapture with a woman who made my soul expand like Lycra.

We talked for hours that seemed like minutes and it took us forever to even look at the pictures, and when she did look she reacted to every one of them, feeling the emotion in each shot. Then she met Wolfe and was mouthing behind her hand to us so he wouldn't hear and be embarrassed, "He's so beautiful!"

When I saw her for the first time at the wedding we both fell into each other's gaze and started

laughing at the beauty of it all. She and I are alike;
we both laugh when emotions run so high they
knock you over with a pogo stick. Her dress was
so intricate and heavy with beads that I was
breathless just staring at her and we kept laughing
and being in the moment of right now with an
open heart, ready for anything that happened.
Then I noticed her mother standing by and told
her, "Jillian is so beautiful, I'm just going to love
looking at her all day!"

Jillian, the girl of my dreams. I've been requesting God to send me a new, wild and raw woman to
love and I got what I wanted. A package of incom-
parable beauty, a laughing, penetrating, articulate
angel who plays violin for a living. Wow.

I loved watching her get married to the groom,
a tall man with lovely fingers and a big heart and
sonorous smooth voice. He asked me, "Do we just
cut the cake or does someone say something right
now or do we do something?" I said, no, just cut
the cake. And then he says the most eloquent toast
about her. "Jillian is the most joy-filled person
inside, the most beautiful woman, and I'm looking
forward to spending the rest of my life with her."
Oh my God. That was my sentiment exactly.

Right before he married her he was at the
church door, raring to go, listening to the organ

music, wanting to be out there at the altar, poised between marriage and being single. I said to him, "I love Jillian!" And he wistfully and simply said, "I love her too."

I hurried to greet the bride again waiting with her bridesmaids and Dad at the back of the church. "You're beautiful!" she told her sister before she strode down the 90-foot aisle. Then the trumpets were sounding and the bride and her father awaited the huge wooden church doors to be flung open. "Have fun," I told her, as if she needed reminding.

The ceremony cascaded from horns to violin to piano to organ, and at the front of the church they vowed to stay married the rest of their lives under those huge stained-glass windows and angels holding up the rotunda. The same church that her parents were married in. They were so excited to be married that they flew up the aisle and I barely kept up with them while I cried into my Hasselblad at the sheer ecstasy of their race towards marriage. I was not going to be trampled so I yelled, "You were running," and Jillian said, "Oh, I'm sorry," and I said, "I loved your running," even though I was skipping backwards, about to fall down from crying and laughing at the same time. That's what I liked about it. That I was transported to another plateau while seeing two lovers unite in wedded bliss.

And then it got even better when we took them to their room and we saw that they had gotten the honeymoon suite! Oh my God, the best room in the hotel and why? Because Sheri the manager loves them. They ran around the room saying, "Oh my God, the honeymoon suite!" And the flower girl and ring bearer were shouting, "Look at the bathtub! Did you see the two decks?" Jillian was laughing at the enormity of it all and I just basked in her glowing.

Then her groom picked her up at the door like it was nothing. Just lifted her in the air and held her aloft to the heavens and I was out of film and had to reload. Cheez.

He swept her up again with a smile and, really, I just wanted to tuck them in bed; the day had been too long for them. Right after getting married they said to me, "Can't we have the reception another day?"

That's how it should be. It's so much effort to get married that really, I told them, they should have a nap right now. But no, they went on to be photographed for as long as we wanted them. And I kept feeling unlimited about our time even though the next photographer was breathing down my neck and the church-chat lady was saying, "You only have five minutes to do twenty minutes worth of pictures." But we got everything and I did even more black-and-white photos, since I was in such actual awe over her elegance and grace that I wanted the nuances of her heart on film forever.

I was walking on air for hours. Every time I looked at her I felt ebullient. They heartily insisted we join them for dinner and said, "Get in there!" with joy in their voices. I felt loved and acknowledged and understood. They even kept saying, "Wolfe is so beautiful!" Finally, I am being loved the way I've always wanted to be.

And that is what success is.

Jillian said, "My family wants to adopt you!" And I said, "I need to be adopted!"

With friends like her I don't need drugs. She's so unabashedly ecstatic that I just want to curl up with her for hours. She invited us to her house for a barbecue the next day. "I'd be honored if you came." We can't, I whined, but it was because we had romantic plans and since I just fell in love with her I was thinking of changing them so I could be with her. But we'd been waiting years for Wolfe to be invited away on a weekend with friends and we really had to do something horny together. It was a tough decision. I felt torn by my new love affair.

It was a lot of ecstasy to inhale all at once, my cup running over, my heart bursting like a freight train, puffing up hills and then free-falling gleefully down again.

I saw God in Jillian's eyes. She lives in Santa Fe and I know I'll be going there to see her. I can't stay away.

I'm in love again. With a gal whose laughing sounds like naughty, mischievous angels always at the ready to soar away on a cloud of joy for the sole reason of having tired face muscles and sore tummies from laughing so hard.

The Metaphysics
of Marriage

Men Don't Snore:
A Navigational Guide
for Marriage

൭ Men don't snore until you videotape them doing it and then they say, "I usually don't sound that way."

Husbands believe that the cold, warm and hot settings on the washing machine are just there to jazz up the controls. The buttons have nothing to do with them personally.

It is not advisable to refrain from meeting one's future in-laws before the wedding. Do so at your own peril.

I had no idea what I was getting into and did it anyway. After getting married I discovered that my husband's mother glues rhinestone pins into naked mannequins and then decorates her lavish home with these treasures. His father dates younger chicks even though he's married and he rides twenty-one motorcycles, but not at the same time.

Husbands think that children can feed themselves after the age of two months and they retire from the kitchen because they have really important projects to work on, like reading their e-mail and surfing the Internet.

Men are known to show up with diamonds couched in velvet-lined boxes so we forget about all of the above.

The remote control is carefully fought over at our house. Then we lose it in the sofa pillows and curse our way out of the cushions to turn the channel. I am the only one to always return the remote to its proper location on top of the VCR. I am the one person in the family who is genetically capable of this small feat.

If I try to clean the car my husband will tell me how to do it. I have to preface the act by saying, "Don't tell me how to wash the car."

Women can produce whole human beings out of their own bodies, but men assume that they are better because they can open the ketchup bottle when it's frozen shut.

Men who bathe regularly can be forgiven for a lot
of things, like not asking for directions when
you've crossed the state line into Oregon and you
were originally headed for Santa Monica.

Men and cars. I know my husband is upset when
his favorite car from the sixties arrives home on a
tow truck. It's a lot worse than my son failing to
do his homework and going to bed without brushing his teeth. His car is very closely connected to
his self-esteem. He believes that if the starter on
his car needs replacing, that means he's a
spineless dog who does not deserve any love at all.

My man believes that cleaning the house will allow
more creativity to flow throughout the ethers of
our home. It usually results in profuse sweating
and a nice long sit-down in his favorite chair
where he reads his e-mail.

Men don't notice that children need six meals a
day and, that if left to their own devices, would eat
KitKats around the clock. Then my guy says to the
young steward of our home, "Don't eat so much
candy—your teeth will fall out."

Men like sex but forget that women need a luxury suite to do it in so they don't have to listen to their children snore while performing. This does not bother men, who can have sex in a parked car on a busy street or in a bedroom that shares a wall with their in-laws.

Women are not built this way. We don't like listening to our fathers snore as we have sex with our husbands. I particularly don't enjoy my mother walking in on me when I'm having sex with my legal husband and saying, "I just need to get something out of the closet"

My husband knew what he was getting into marrying me but I had no idea that his sister would be pressing us to make stew out of my placenta after our child was born.

It is better not to offer advice, even if asked about how to raise children that are not yours. When your new nephew is ripping your silk curtains, peeing on your rug, teasing your dog and asking for a quick meal right now—a burrito would do nicely— and then running through your house with it, it is better to just move out of state. That way you'll never have to see the little urchin again.

Men are very fragile. You have to make them believe that it was their idea to take out the trash or they will go into their caves and sulk until the weekend. Then they will come out and want to fool around.

I like being married. This way I can talk to other men without them thinking that I want to go to bed with them. Even if I did daydream about it a little.

Men think it's better to schedule sex than to just let it happen naturally. That way they can read their e-mail and wash the car with gusto, knowing that later on, before they fall asleep and start not snoring, they will be getting what they think about 100% of the time.

Women think about sex less often. They are too busy earning money and worrying about their children's dental health. The thought of braces is highly upsetting to a woman's peace of mind.

Women have to be in the mood. Men get in the mood by not engaging in any meaningful conversation with their women and then collapsing exhausted on the bed.

Women like surprises. Men like to surprise us with a carefully planned itinerary to our favorite honeymoon spot, arranged by us.

The brides always tell me, "He's in charge of the honeymoon." And I think, that's the last time he'll be calling for airline tickets just to get her in bed.

Hey! You men out there, prove me wrong!
I'm waiting.

Melting at the Knees

᏶ Women often tell me, "You're so lucky to have Michael. How did you ever find him?"

What they don't want to hear is how I found myself before I met him. How I fell in love with me first and traveled the planet, dancing in bars, walking on beaches, laughing hard with friends and eating in restaurants alone.

I'd had so many substitutes for a real boyfriend that I just gave them up entirely and decided to ride my bike instead while noticing the landscape of my own soul. I was putting all my focus on cute guys and none on myself. I wanted to fall in love with me.

After every doomed love affair I found myself on the ground again, my knees melted under me, lying in a pool of my own dreams. A pool of my own beauty and wondering why he wasn't the one again, and it probably had something to do with the way I didn't measure up to his standards as a lover.

I was trying to make this guy with the God-chiseled hands be the father of my children and light my fire at the same time. This guy who would rather tinker with his Riviera on weekends.

So I thought I'd just stay down there and not stand up again. I'd stay melted, soft and squishy and tender, revealing the naked parts of me that I was trying to hide from public view.

I started to pray more. I was on my knees, after all. I was one of those pilgrims, crawling along through the streets towards falling in love with myself and I wasn't going to get up until I found out how great I was. Who was I, anyway?

See, women don't find men to love. When you look for a man to love you, you don't find one. There's a hunting-for-prey look on the face. I know. I had one emblazoned on mine before I decided to stay in the prayer position. Being raised Catholic helped. For once.

I noticed couples in love, kissing on the MUNI bus, walking down the street, sitting and laughing in restaurants, and I began to be happy for them. The world needs lovers and just because I didn't have someone right then didn't mean I wasn't good enough.

I wanted to take a train ride on my own soul.

I even cut down on flirting and my knock-men-over-with-a-look looks.

Well... I did look when they weren't looking.

I even gave up sex alone. I'd get all worked up
with my own hand and there was no one to tango
with. It felt emotionally bankrupt. So I quit that
too. Now I had lots of time to just be with myself
and ride trains across America and stay down
there on my bloody knees, healing up a storm that
had been brewing for years in my heart because I
couldn't quite find the right lap to fill.

After about ten months I almost broke down
and wanted to fall in love again with an inappro-
priate boy-man. I scared him off by bringing him
flowers one day. That's all it took.

And then a few days later I met Michael. He
found me right after my Halloween party at a bar
ordering a vodka, after watching me dance wildly
and sweatily with my friends in a place where people just drink and do not dance. He found me. God
sent him. I did not find him.

I was immediately attracted to him from forty
paces down the length of the bar as I looked up
and saw him staring into my soul so deeply, he
saw all the way to Saturn and back. For the first
time in my life I looked into a man's eyes and did-
n't want to hide anything. Then I turned away and
sat down with my friends. I didn't go running up
to him like the old me would have done, the one
who dispensed with formalities and began kissing

guys before they found out my name and birth-date.

He came and sat down at my table and asked me in my costume and face paint, "Are you schizo-phrenic?" and I knew he wanted to know who I was underneath the facade that I showed the world. "Yeah, how did you know?" I asked, with my face painted in two halves of black and white theater paint, striped down the middle of my nose.

I wasn't lucky. I just gave up substandard love affairs featuring great sex and nothing else or poor sex and nothing else. I gave it all up for Lent so I would recognize my true love when I saw him.

That's what happened eighteen years ago. We're still together and we're still growing up and realizing that it's never easy. We've had fights, yelled at each other, considered divorce and left the house, slamming the door. Love is not for the faint of heart.

When I hear women say they are jealous of me, I want to say that if they feel that way they aren't ready for the salmon-swimming-against-the-current nature of being in love. It isn't all easy and perfect. And tidy without mess. Love isn't for sissies or for folks who want the other person to do all the work so they can play squash and take over companies and be important and complain to their friends about the opposite sex and be too busy to laugh with their partner because they have to make these calls right now.

You have to be willing to be nailed naked to the cross of love. Baring the cellulite and all the private parts we'd rather not have poked and prodded.

And that's how he found me. Covered in theater paint and dancing in a bar. Who would have thunk it?

How to Choose a Husband

ᕦ Why is it that our friends and family just up and marry whomever they want to without consulting us?

If only they had listened to me, their lives would be far more carefree and I would visit them more often.

I'm not mentioning any names here because I don't want to have to call my lawyer again today; it's expensive. The guilty never recognize themselves anyway.

I have a relative who won't accept a job unless the new company can pay for every last bit of his hypochondria dementia. When I visit him I'm asked to buy groceries as soon as I step off the plane and help clean out the attic because his back hurts. So much for throwing out the welcome mat. It's real red-carpet treatment. You want to kill yourself before the visit is over just so you can bleed on his rug.

Then there's another relative who hasn't learned my last name yet, even though it's the same one that his wife used to wear. It's only been twenty years that they've been married; maybe after another twenty he'll figure out who I am.

I've got news for them. Here's how to pick a guy to spend the rest of your life with.

Make sure he is fully employed. If you support him he'll expect cooked-to-order meals too. I can't stress this enough.

Is he crazy about you or just crazy? It's so much better to hook up with a guy who doesn't require mental hospitalization. Try for sane.

Does he call you or just say he will? Don't freeze out your gal pals because he might call tonight for a date. You are very busy visiting prisons and playing the stock market and eating Mars Bars to just stop what you're doing and wriggle into a short dress.

Make sure he's over his last lover. Old-girlfriend stories where he waxes poetic over her salami lasagna are irritating.

Just try to find a guy without kids; it's damn near impossible.

Forget about liking his family; you won't. It's unrealistic to expect the open-arms treatment from them when they'd just as soon open arms on you for taking away their son.

If he buys you things like blenders and vacuum

bags for your birthday, he isn't crazy about you. When a man is truly in love he will do anything to get in your pants. Even waiting for you to be ready. He'll buy you jewelry, lacy bits of underwear that aren't big enough to blow his nose in, but he will try to and even make you homemade cards. Cast-iron pans and flannel nightgowns are a sure sign that his rocker arms need gapping. Meaning his carburetor is not firing fuel the way it should.

Sex. If you want to do it more than he does, this is not good. It sounds grandmotherish but let him lead in the romance department. That way you'll know if he's really interested in you. You can trail perfume, dress come-hitherly and have a complete set of silk teddies, but if you jump his bones first he'll be turned off. He wants to get you into bed valiantly by sounding the battle cry of sexual conquest across the fruited plains.

This took me decades to figure out.

As soon as they know you'll open your legs any time any where, the thrill is gone for them. Men's conquest clocks tick harder if you let them initiate sex. You both get laid, so what difference does it make if he starts it?

Do you want a man or a meal ticket? Don't marry someone rich so you can pursue your art full-time. You will end up pursuing tennis bracelets, manicures and the bottle. Idle money that you did not earn makes you smug and lazy. You start wondering why people buy Toyotas rather than BMWs. Ask yourself, would I marry him if he wasn't rich?

Does he act all winded over gorgeous women in your presence? It's fine to admire a firm butt or two, but no heavy salivating and panting in front of you. Even when you've been married for decades, you want to think that you are the most beautiful babe on the planet to him.

Flirting. I like to be flirted with, even by my own lover. Flirting is spontaneous and fun. It lets you know that he's interested and keeps zestiness in the liaison. If he flirts with you now, he'll still be chasing you around the house in twenty years.

He must know how to kiss well. I don't think they can be trained to do this like the other sex things. Kissing is innate. I've read books on how to kiss, but I'm convinced that the spirit behind a kiss is more important than the physical razzle-dazzle of the lips. Tongues slide from a place deep within the soul. It cannot be taught to slobbering boors and ineffectual peckers. Cadence and rhythm of lovemaking can be learned but not something as earth shattering as a great kiss. Kissing tells you how the man will be in bed. If his kisses are slow, tantalizing and lingering, that's how he'll be between the sheets. If he's in a hurry, can't calm down or looks at his watch, move onto the next.

Here's the most important tip. He must make you laugh or the marriage won't last. When your teenager drives the car into the side of the house and you are considering bankruptcy and all of your son's friends are using your driveway for a skateboard ramp while you try to have sex on the other side of the wall, it is critical that you laugh during these moments. Nothing kills romance faster than the permanent refusal to laugh at ourselves and the neighbors and the kids and the boss. Try to keep a laugh under your belt so you don't need a belt.

You might think I'm overly critical but we're talking marriage here. Not just some casual sex over cappuccino. Not some frantic fling over 4th of July weekend because you're horny.

This is forever-and-ever stuff.

Wedding from Hell

ꚍ Everything was all set for the big day until we had to change the wedding date six days before the nuptials.

There was one small thing. Michael's divorce wasn't final. We sheepishly approached my father, who replied, "The judge has to chase you down the aisle with the divorce papers!"

In New York State it is considered bad form to marry if you are already detained in matrimony with a previous wife. Michael tried explaining this to his lawyer, but instead of filing the necessary papers, she just moved across town and lost his request in the flurry.

At least this would give me a few more days to finish the nightmare of a wedding dress I was sewing. Talk about hell. Somewhere in my pea brain I had this firmly entrenched notion that I had to do everything for my wedding except sign my fiancé's divorce papers.

I had wrestled with nine yards of silk for my wedding dress that was patched together like a quilt on LSD, and when it was done it didn't fit. I

slipped it over my head and stopped breathing.
The wind had been knocked out of my trachea. It
needed to be let out but there was nowhere for it
to go. After beating my fists on the walls, I added
another band of silk around the empire waist and
proceeded to screw up the baking of my wedding
cake.

This is a job that should only be handled by
professionals. I for one do not know how to convert a cake recipe for 300 people into a wittily iced
cake for twenty. I tried to cover up my mistake
with rows of strawberries but it didn't work.
Rather than serving two layers of deflated styrofoam to my guests, I decided to slip a Duncan
Hines layer under one of the styrofoam slabs and
call it a day. This was after my third attempt at getting my cake to rise.

I inspected the cake plates after the guests had
left. Only the layer made from scratch was left on
the dishes. Duncan Hines won.

I had other troubles. The exact timing of the
deli platter from Wegman's was a concern. Would
there be enough luncheon meat with the covered
dish of lasagna my friend was bringing to serve
twenty people? My father was worried about
bologna and I was battling with braiding my hair
into birdnests above my ears. I hadn't discovered

hair spray yet. Finally I just put it in a bun and should have had a stiff one but I didn't drink doubles then. It would have been an ideal day to start.

Then Grandma called to say she was too sick to come to the wedding. "I've got diarrhea, Mary." So did I but that didn't stop me from going to my own wedding. I think it was all those cakes that I baked.

I had a feeling my grandmother's diarrhea had something to do with my aunt visiting her. Sister Fidalia was a full-fledged nun who had been incarcerated since the age of eleven in a convent without benefit of fresh bread or sex. She would always arrive at Grandma's house with a huge bag of stale bread and cake from Harrison Bakery, across from the convent. She had once brought a cake shaped like an open Bible which Grandma had shellacked to admire forever. That's probably what got Grandma feeling all mushy inside.

Michael and I leaped into our rusting van with grenade impressions on the quarter panels and drove out to Grandma's house on the way to the wedding. I slipped into my nine yards of homemade dress in the cabin of our beleaguered van in the sweaty afternoon of a June day in Syracuse. The silk stuck to my skin as I looked through the holes in the van at Grandma's house. She appeared at the front door looking pissed that we had showed up. She looked fine to me, but then Grandma could be suffering from severe psoriasis and be dragging out fully loaded trash cans to the curb in a blizzard. That's why I thought a little diarrhea shouldn't stop her from attending something as important as my wedding. Her face went white and it wasn't from losing her lunch. Her greeting still rings in my ears. "What are you doing here?" she bellowed.

The stony silence of the living room welcomed me as I twirled in my stitched and dyed finery. Grandma and Sister Fidalia both looked like they had been eating stale cake from Harrison's. Sister Fidalia wasn't coming to the church because the ceremony was non-Catholic. This made me a pagan in her eyes.

She had removed her wimple and was sitting in her favorite chair at Grandma's house, clucking her disapproval. Michael tried to kiss her and she waved him off with a "yah, yah, yah." I got the feeling that we had interrupted the flinging of gossip about our wedding and they needed to get right back to it. Grandma said, "Go. Go to your wedding!"

Well, first we had to get some flowers, which just happened to be growing on the side of the road as we careened towards the church. Thank goodness for those wild sweet peas! Now all we had to do was get married without the car breaking down on the way, and if you had seen the car you would doubt that it could transport anything as precious as living human beings. The last owner used our van for the conveying of corpses on the way to a funeral home from the hospital. Which is exactly where Michael found the engagement ring that he gave me. A silver ring that had probably rolled off a dead woman's hand while being delivered to the funeral home. It gets better.

We arrived at the church in our van that had a two-by-four for a bumper. Let's see, there were seven guests, counting the church secretary, and none of them were here yet. This was not feeling really special.

The minister was an authentic babe who had been our personal guru for months. She had told us after our first conference with her, "Wear your blue jeans to church when you come." We were way impressed with this. I didn't own a dress and Michael hadn't seen the inside of a suit since childhood. She liked us more than our own parents did.

In lieu of payment for services rendered we gave her a ceramic bowl that Michael had made and $10. She accepted this without a whimper.

She had never mentioned money. I didn't know that brides and grooms actually pay the minister for performing a ceremony.

My parents showed and looked tense in their finery. They hadn't been in a non-Catholic church since before they were born so they wanted to bolt. Nanna, my other grandmother, was there which really flattered me since she had ridden a bus from Buffalo to get there. She behaved beautifully until after the cake was cut when she snapped at me, "Why weren't you married in the Catholic church?" and "Why didn't your father walk you down the aisle?"

So there we were. About to get married. I told my father that he and my mother would walk behind Michael and me down the aisle. Hey, later on I found out Bruce Springsteen did the same thing so I don't know why it was such a slap in the face.

"He's not wearing shoes!" Dad cried out in anguish.

We just couldn't find any shoes for Michael that were a blend of Woodstock and wingtips, so he just went shoeless. We marched rigidly up the aisle and stopped at the altar. So this was it? Sue Ellen dispensed with the formalities in minutes, quoting Kahlil Gibran and moving on to our vows at lightning speed. She probably had somewhere to go.

Michael had written a whole three-act play for his vows and was sobbing through them, when I realized that my idea of just saying my vows off the cuff was not going to fly. All of my friends—well, two of them, anyway—started crying while I just kept thinking that his wedding clothes had turned out better than mine. I had sewn those too, in between agonizing over when his divorce would be final and wondering when to tell Grandma that the man I was marrying was already married but was going to be available really soon. So I told Michael to tell her and she had said, "I thought that was all over!" Apparently someone had leaked it to her or she just had a brain like a sonogram.

My vows were, I'll love you in any kind of weather, and I think that was it. Then we were officially married and I got to kiss him through his tears and listen to my father harumph behind me in the pew. I just couldn't cry with my father sighing heavily behind my silken back.

You know that feeling of relief everyone gets when a wedding is over? Well, it didn't happen at mine. There was high-voltage tension radiating from my family. On the other side of the pews were my two friends Debbie and Joy, who were

still crying, and the church secretary in the back
was sobbing into her Kleenex. Thank God someone remembered the Chopin tape. It broke up the
chill and made it freezing. Sue Ellen wanted to
close up the church. She bustled us out in her tai-
lored suit and waved gaily good-bye.

The boys in our neighborhood had decorated
our morgue van! It was festooned with crepe paper
and love. The high point of the day. Except for the
horn getting stuck in honk mode and blasting con-
tinuously as we drove to my parents' house for a
reception of bologna and deflated cake.

Things started loosening up at the party. My
father poured lower-grade whiskey into an upscale
bottle and sat with his cronies in the kitchen, looking relieved that Barnum and Bailey had closed
down the circus for the day. My mother was wring-
ing her hands wondering if I was still Catholic or
not and Grandma greeted us at the front door,
snapping, "Why didn't your father walk you down
the aisle?" followed by, "Why didn't you get married in the Catholic church?"

I opened my gifts. The stackable wooden blocks
that spelled out LOVE would really brighten someone's kitsch collection now. And the blue blanket
from my aunt shredded when I washed it. My
mother gave me an ironing board and some ugly

stainless that she didn't need anymore. Service for eight. We were on our way now.

For the wedding night we passed out on Joy and Jimmy's futon across from their bedroom and didn't have sex. The room echoed and after flaking Michael off of me and denouncing the idea of sex with an attentive audience, we fell asleep. Nothing has changed.

Sixteen years later I still don't want to have sex when I'm tired or know for sure that Wolfe hasn't fallen asleep yet. Maybe in another decade we'll get this right.

Maybe right after menopause.

How to Seduce
Your Husband

Ꮗ I am not talking Frederick's of Hollywood here.
I'm talking about loving yourself so much that he
can't resist you as you walk through the room on
your way to the bathroom.

Here's what I've learned after being married for
sixteen years. You can't live his life for him, gals.
You can't tell him what to do and improve him.
But. You can be so mesmerizing that he can't
stand being away from you.

First. You really should get rid of all your ripped
panties. Wearing dainty lacy handkerchief undies
from Ireland does help in the bedroom. No, you
don't have to purchase crotchless thongs if you like
the feeling of a fabric-free crack. The thing is you
will feel sexy and that is the main reason for wearing them. You know the $26 panties are under
your sweatpants and that makes you excited,
right? Wear them at your own peril.

Enough about undies.

The real path to seduction has nothing to do
with meeting him at the door naked, although I

don't want to discourage you from doing so. It's
just that when you finally decide to do it, he'll be
bringing home his boss for dinner as a surprise
and you'll be foaming at the mouth when you see
them at the front door, not to mention bone-
chillingly cold.

Really. Here it is, the honest-to-God truth. You
have to love yourself so much that you'd never
succumb to someone's negative assessment of
you. It's that simple. If you waver on this basic
fact, you will not find Mr. Right. You have to know
you're amazing without anyone agreeing with you.
It's the only way. And have you noticed? The world
loves people like Richard Avedon who show up
and say, "I'm here, now get out of my way." It's
just confidence, nothing more.

Today, the limo driver at work said to me out of
the blue, "I loved your coming-out show."

Say what?

He said, "You look just like Ellen Degeneres."

Personally, I think I'm better looking and was
surprised that he hadn't noticed. Her salary I'd like
but not her nose. And he expected me to be
flattered. That guy would never get a date with me.

But back to seduction.

Getting lit up about anything is the prescription
for horny rolls in the hay. When I get flame points

in my eyes I'm so alive that I feel like a hand grenade. And I just know I'm damn sexy too. When I'm all deflated about my overdue bills, I'm on my way to an early grave. I just don't have time to be happy; I'm too busy being angry at the world for not providing me with a new red Lincoln Continental. My clients have nice houses—why can't I? I whine.

Seduction involves thinking past Nasdaq, politics and in-laws who make your teeth ache. It's sort of like being a kid again when nothing really mattered all that much because at night you had a warm bed to fall into that parents paid the rent on. Worries were non-habit-forming episodes involving being mad at your sister because she got the window in the car and you had to sit in the middle, breathing her stale air.

So. You know you're sexy, right? There's no question about it. Not in any fiber of your being are you worried that your hips are too big and your brain is too small. You have to know this. Because then it doesn't matter how much you weigh. I've seen plenty of gals who tip the scale mightily, with devoted men wrapped around their ardor. These women don't give a fig what their poundage is and neither do their blissed-out husbands. See? They know something. They know they are sexy.

I'm not saying you'll never hit a few dry spells in your life. Particularly when the sexual frontier is bone dry as a desert, you must know the truth with all your heart. Even when there is no one lapping at your private parts, it just means that you haven't given them a chance. You're far too busy saving the planet or finishing your carton of Häagen-Dazs or grooming your pet poodle or visiting prisons. Whatever.

You have a life. And you're not giving it up for some unemployed permanent couch fixture.

So. You're in love with yourself. Now it's time to waft some perfume down the hall after you walk by his cave and notice that he's available right now, but you don't have to say a word. He has smelled you coming and now, since you've been too busy at your yoga class and upholstery lessons and lead-singing with a rock group, you just don't have that much time to simply fuck anymore. It's more like when you were dating and he couldn't see you every day.

Trust me, this works.

Just be sure the kids are asleep before you rip off each other's clothes and slide into a hypnotic sex trance.

If you can't wait, then just stuff some underwear in your mouth so they won't hear you.

Domestic Servitude

෧ I don't know what possessed me to clean out
the silverware drawer this morning. All of a sudden
those plastic forks, carefully stored by the gross
next to the ancient packets of catsup, sent me over
the edge.

I wanted to throw out everything that is useless
in my life.

It was thrilling to unceremoniously fling those
twenty-odd plastic forks in the trash with barely a
passing thought of "I should be recycling." Then,
with ill-disguised disgust, the catsup packets
followed the forks.

Now I was looking at a crumb-coated drawer.
For some reason I wanted to clean it. Standing
there in my bathrobe, avoiding my morning
writing, I dove in with gusto. Cleaning the outside
of the drawer, I noticed a wood-grain pattern that
was similar to how it looked when we first bought
this chopping-block table ten years ago. Covered in
grime for years? I had forgotten how pretty the
drawer pulls were.

Michael is concerned about his hernia operation. Not for medical reasons but for how he's

going to be able to cope with my lack of enthusiasm for daily cleaning. I can gaily walk by food puddles on the kitchen floor with a devil-may-care attitude, never stopping to consider that I could do anything to rescue this linoleum in search of a mop. I know that the dust kitties and crumbs on the hardwood floors are bothering him, but I just carefully wipe my feet off before getting into bed with him at night.

"What do you want, a housemaid or a seductress?"

Sometimes he doesn't get either one, but I do take far more pride in my silk teddy collection than my perfectly organized linen closet. I know too many people who emphasize the clean floors over the sex and their husbands don't look too happy about it.

I'd much rather loll naked in cracker crumbs on the bed than spend the same amount of time vacuuming. He can't have it both ways.

I'm looking forward to seeing him lie back after his operation and not be able to clean anything. When we first met I was surprised to find that he jumped up to wash dishes after every meal. I thought he was just showing off to impress me but he's still doing it eighteen years later, when he should be just reading the paper after dinner.

It's like comparing a mountaintop with the foothills. You can see much further into the true nature of things if you just refrain from unnecessary activities like washing dishes and floors. There are so many more available hours to do something worthwhile if you don't clutter up your life with useless chores. The kitchen floor never stays clean like the words on a page do after writing them. I just can't get too excited about an activity I'm going to have to repeat all the time, so why not wait until the kitchen floor really needs to be cleaned, like at Christmas?

I have my hands full because Wolfe wants to eat at regular intervals throughout the day, as if I don't have anything else to do.

But this morning I got a thrill out of seeing my drawer front clean. There have even been a few fleeting seconds where I considered vacuuming the floors, because I know it would put a smile on the big guy's face and he's been kind of low lately, thinking about his gut being cut open next week. I'm looking around the bedroom now and each corner has snowdrifts of dust that are surely grating on his senses. But the doctor said he's not supposed to lift anything heavier than a six-pack.

Can he drink it after he picks it up?

Right now he's disgruntled about the layers of

crust on the refrigerator shelves. I blithely keep
covering them up with new groceries. Who can see
the crust with tomatoes and milk blocking the
view? He doesn't like that reasoning, but he knows
that he's supposed to be "cutting back" before his
surgery and releasing little chores, like washing the
car, cleaning out the basement and making the
windows sparkle before retiring for the night. He
is dismayed by our lack of enthusiasm when it
comes to mopping floors and keeping clutter out
of sight.

"Papa, you're not supposed to be cleaning!"
Wolfe sternly admonishes him. "Papa" goes right
on rinsing the dishes and stacking the dishwasher.
Then, I see him down on the kitchen floor,
scraping up last week's menu. I want him to rest
easy so he doesn't have any more hernia attacks
and so he can photograph our two weddings this
weekend with me.

I wish we could go ahead and get the surgery
done this week, but we had to schedule it around
our weddings and they're already paid in full.
They're expecting two photographers to show up
and they don't have to know that one of them is
wearing a truss. I don't want him wasting his
energy cleaning the floor when he should be saving it for carrying the Hasselblad on Saturday.

I know he would love it if I was more interested in domestic duties. But I have my priorities right—no housework before creative work; hugging and kissing in the middle of the day on the bed is better than hanging up the wash. Crusty refrigerator shelves are a fact of life. There is nothing wrong with shirking the dust kitties when I have something more important to do, like write a book or do some filmmaking or even walk the dog.

I believe in preventative mental health over a clean house. He likes to have everything sparkly clean before he sits down to work. I want him to rest easy while he recuperates from surgery, but I know he'll be wondering when the grime will be peeled off the hardwood floors and how he can live much longer walking on Wolfe's breakfast crumbs in the kitchen. I have even thought of calling in a housecleaning service for his recovery. That way, I don't have to knock myself out trying to do it all, as in cooking and maintaining a Florence Nightingale veneer. That's enough work for me.

He must have thought I was neat when we first started courting. The only reason I had a clean house was that I got bored waiting for him to show, so I'd spruce the place up until he got there. He should have known what he was getting into when he caught me sweeping my rugs with a broom. I didn't own a vacuum cleaner until he moved in.

He's been quite cheerful about my high standards of dust tolerance. He has never offered to trade me in for a more domestic model down the street. After eighteen years he has accepted the fact that I'm not getting more interested in controlling crust buildup in my refrigerator. He doesn't complain much when he sees my shoes all over the house. I've even noticed him leaving his shoes out of the closet now and then. And there are times when I break down and clean the bathtub. I draw the line at the toilet, though.

We have our little quirks that have been tolerated over the years, but we've never had surgery performed on either one of us and then had to lie in bed without moving.

I really don't know how I'm going to keep him from washing the dishes and cleaning the windows. I've succeeded in refusing to let him carry out the garbage and doing the vacuuming, so I am winning somewhat.

Now if I can just get him to stay away from the kitchen floor.

On the Verge
of Being
a Grown-up

Full Throttle at Forty

வ "You look good for forty." This is what I'm hearing now when I proudly proclaim my spot in the linear lineup of birthdays. It's how long I've been on the planet inside this particular body. A longitudinal reference point in time connected to another birthday, so big deal.

People are not sure how to respond when I sound happy about turning forty. So they tell me I look younger. But this is how forty looks, folks! I'm not well preserved like canned pickles and apricot jam; I just laugh a lot. And I haven't died while still being alive. The more I relax the less I care what someone thinks of me and the more I enjoy eating ice cream and spaghetti loaded with meatballs. I breathe all the way down to my toenails and beyond. I feel young.

Even twenty-year-olds can go dead before they expire. It's a light-in-the-eyes kind of thing. When the sparkles go out from behind the retinas, it's time for a wake-up call. If there's no enthusiasm in life, get a jump start; it's that simple. Stop whining and try something so unfamiliar it makes your knees knock in a staccato beat. That'll do it.

I feel younger now than when I was twenty-two. I thought I knew so much then. Now I know how much I don't know. And what I do know can fit in a sugar bowl compared to what my kid knows.

I was more cynical as a youngster of twenty than I am now at forty. I still get angry at evil but I'm learning how not to let it spoil my date tonight with loverman. I'm learning how to live in a world that has both. I don't like the fact that my kid's bedroom looks like the stirred-up dust from the lunar landing and that lawyers are necessary and sexual predators roam the planet, but I'm not going to go to bed for the rest of my life over these facts.

Just since last week I'm yelling less. If you don't believe me, ask the men that I live with. I've been trying to train them for years and sometimes they don't like it. Imagine that. This is why I'm going to therapy now.

Michael resisted the counseling idea, maintaining that a date at a white-tablecloth restaurant would be much more invigorating for the marriage, but now that he's actually going with me, he just kicks his heels like a draft horse rearing up and goes along with it. He's not ecstatic about it like I am but change is hard; it doesn't happen overnight.

It's all part of my "Get Over It" slogan as I round the bend of my fourth decade here on earth. Instead of worrying about bankruptcy, poverty and holes in my attitude, why not just let it all go, get over it. There's so much more to be thankful, curious and enthusiastic about.

It takes so little to get my groove back.

Just driving our 1985 Suburban this morning made me feel rich. I don't care that it's a gas-guzzling pig on steroids; I feel like a queen in it. My bucket seat is plush. I can't get over what it feels like to drive a car that doesn't have shredded upholstery and crumbling carpets. Now all we have to do is pay for it.

Am I creeping towards being comfortable? Not with my debt. Or maybe comfort is a state of mind. I must be forty, talking about being comfortable.

But I'm glad to be forty. I don't need to be told that I really don't look bad for being so ancient. Why not live life to the fullest and try joy on for size?

Joy doesn't have an age limit. Laughing isn't just for kids; curiosity is an underused faculty.

Why? Because people don't want to learn anything
new. The boundaries around the brainpan spring
up, forcing out the new, the different, the challenging. I see it in the glazed-over attitude of the fur-
coat set, the humdrum among us who won't take
any risks, myself included, when I'm all shut down
and my heart shrinks to the size of a walnut.
Sitting in my Barcalounger, using the remote on
my brain.

This is not good.

I'm living more pedal to the metal now. I'm not
going to sit home while Anthony Hopkins, at age
sixty-eight, drives up and down the California
coast in his Plymouth while I read about it in *Pre-
miere* magazine. I'm only forty. I've got a lot of
adventures to fly and a low-riding Plymouth Fury
to drive.

In my twenties I lived life without a rudder
and didn't fasten my seat belt. I didn't know I
could do anything. I had dreams of being an
actress, a filmmaker, a photographer, a writer, but
didn't delve into those disciplines with the passion
of a seagoing vessel churning across the Atlantic,
the Queen Elizabeth voyaging to Europe.

I'm more excited now to explore my person-
hood, femininity, soul than ever before. I pickax
the ice, shattering my assumptions, letting my true

self out. Now that I'm forty I grab a sledgehammer and swing away with gusto.

I feel more articulate now that I'm not hiding behind a cloud of smoke, dummying up to the truth. Sure, I miss it sometimes, when I want to run naked through the deadness of the world, but I can still do that sober. I am choosing courage now, even when my knees are knocking my windpipes. I am choosing the path that speaks to me rather than asking others' advice. I am cuddling up to myself like cashmere on a cold night. Being my own best friend. I'll always have me to rely on.

I go straight through all the thorny dilemmas, a ship surging through the water, calmly taking the waves, plowing on, my prow boldly pointed forward.

At age twenty, I had such a viewpoint to defend. Now I just don't give a fuck.

I love being with people in the right-now-this-is-moment, not trotting out past achievements and honors. Simply enjoying the freshness of being alive with a person in the now, this is sacred moment. Appreciating the beauty of being able to smell, have sex when we can get it, laugh, plant marigolds, watch Wolfe grow and discover the sparkle in other people's eyes.

Living full throttle, none of this half-mast stuff.

Pubic Hair, Cellulite and Flab

ᐰ I did something dangerous today. I bought an industrial-strength black bikini slit up to my neck with those leg openings that stretch all the way to Idaho.

We D-cup gals have little to choose from. Most bathing suits are made for those who long for breasts and have dimunitive hips that don't jiggle to match.

I gushed when I saw the size 14 bottoms. I knew I had a winner. Why? Because it was big enough to wedge both my lower cheeks into.

I like wearing two-piece bathing suits even though my gut hangs out in ripples. I gave up on a washboard tummy in high school when I figured out how many sit-ups it took to maintain it. And I cringe at the thought of using Neet. I'm hoping no one will notice. And if they do they're looking too closely.

I'm liberated now. I can finally wear a French-cut bikini without worrying about my cellulite. I know it's there. So what?

Parading around in public with my private parts hanging out won't be that bad. I've always had inhibitions but they never did me any good.

I was thrilled to even find a size 14 and clutched it to my bosom before some other big gal noticed and wanted to take it from me. It was the only one in the store. If I hadn't snatched it then, the company would have stopped making them. Whenever I find a suit I like, it immediately stops being manufactured before I get it to the dressing room. So now I head straight for the D-cup rack. It's the only game in town.

I barely glanced at the price—it didn't matter what it cost. It was big enough for my derriere to descend into. Ecstasy!

And my breasts would fit in the top too. I wouldn't be cut off from oxygen by a too small bra that didn't want to meet me in the back at the closure. And we didn't have to special order it like I was a hump-backed gorilla trying to fit inside a Speedo.

Now I just had to fight my way into the dressing room, narrowly missing a gaggle of teenage girls who were inspecting bathing suits with extra padding built in to the bra cups. They don't have breasts; they just need Band-Aids. At least they can run when they want to and not have their breasts hit them in the face.

Oh no, the dressing rooms were full. This could take until the next millennium. I know what those people in there are doing. They are prancing around in front of the mirror, trying to imagine being out in public wearing a few square inches of nylon rather than being safely sequestered in this closet.

Wearing a bathing suit is worse than being naked. Those strips of nylon bellow out to those near and far, "Look at me!" It's hard not to notice when bikini bottoms are slit up to your teeth and the top is roving down, way down the cleavage in that raciest of all the colors in the spectrum—black.

I looked like I was wearing lingerie, not a suitable uniform for swimming laps five times a week. Maybe I should forget the swimming and just use this outfit for sex.

But what am I to do? Speedo suits come in small, medium and extra small large. There's nothing quite like trying on the extra large "grande dame" size and finding out that I can't move my diaphragm, which means I'll need an oxygen tank just to wear it. Great. Another suit that would be perfect for a girl in the eighth grade. I, however, have lived through breast-feeding and have the

stretched-out gut to go with the mammary glands
that were used to nurse Godzilla. Now, try and find
a strip of spandex to cover that shelf.

I looked in the mirror noticing the high-cut legs
first. There was even more pubic hair showing
than the last suit I wore, which took months to get
used to. I am a firm believer in resisting hot wax
on my privates under any circumstances. It
conjures up having each hair individually tweezed
out by the roots, bringing shudders to my pain
threshold.

And for what? It just grows back. No matter
how much lava-like wax you pour over unwanted
hair it shows up again like relatives sleeping on your
couch. I thought I got over this in college when I
gave up shaving for good. Now my best friend tries
to rub out the mustache hair under my nose that
looks like smudges from a hastily eaten meal. This
is her way of telling me I should bleach it.

Now that the bikini bottoms are on my hips
they look even smaller than they did on the
hanger. Should I insist on extra fabric sewn onto
the leg openings or simply brave the stares of
mostly women who look at me like I'm breaking
the rules of depilatory etiquette? So there it was.
Two healthy dollops of hair hanging out on either
side of a barely discernible black bikini bottom. I

had to decide. Was I ready for the viewing public?

My midriff bulge was decoratively draped over the bottoms. This was a new lesson in giving up vanity. Hey! If people were noticing my imperfections, then they weren't looking into my eyes and bothering to see my soul. So let them look at my pubic hair. So what?

I felt better already. It was time to commit. The teenage girls were clawing the door off the dressing room. Yes. I will wear this suit in public. I will pay the amount on the price tag. I will not wait for August when the sales start and there aren't any good suits left in my size.

I burst forth from the dressing room, clutching my two bits of nylon for the price of a nice dinner out.

This getup would work well as bedroom bait too. I was looking forward to pirouetting in it for loverman. He sees my flab and still loves me. As he likes to say, "There's more real estate to love."

Or as my son says, "Lose some weight, Mom."

Hey. Let him go sit on a deck chair on the other side of the pool. I'm going to be bold and wear my new bikini without reservations. It covers almost everything, so what's the big deal?

I will not be imprisoned in a one-piece suit that dramatically hugs my crotch in an unfashionable snuggy. I will never have to pull my bottoms out of my crack. This is freedom.

I bare my bikini-clad body to the world. And bravely release judgment on my loose gut. I am free and I still love myself.

Anything is possible.

Bottle Blonde

෮ I was so sure I didn't want to dye my hair when all of it was brown. Now that spiky white hairs are pointing skyward out of my head, I'm reconsidering.

It would be fun to be a bleached blonde. When I was five I noticed my dark blonde hair officially turn brown and felt deflated. I liked blonde hair. Now, I cut off my hair to a length just above bald. Then the white hairs start arriving like in-laws who drop by without calling first. So I cut them off at the root and dream of being a bottle blonde.

How shallow of me.

Last year I wrote about how gray hair is a badge of honor and all that drivel. How we women have to stick together and not dye our hair just to look glamorous. But hey, I like glamour, me, who has recently shaved my legs for the first time in twenty years. And even my armpits.

I'm beginning to take stock of my assets. Not the financial ones I don't have but the physical ones. The ones that we all judge each other by. Let's face it, I know when a man is reacting to my

nipples and not me. I know when women are
annoyed that I look something close to good. These
are the "friends" I'm replacing. But deeper than
that observation is the feeling of just feeling good
about myself, no matter what.

And I think I'd feel better as a blonde.

I saw a photo of Emma Thompson with blonde
hair and thought, that could be me. Why not? She
is a glamorous, grown-up, a fully functioning, mag-
netic and sparkly forty-year-oldish woman. So what
if she dyes her hair?

Gee. I was so judgmental last year. Before my
gray hair started coming in like a rottweiler's winter coat. It just kept coming, wouldn't stop no
matter how much I cut it. Is this a forty-year-old
midlife semicrisis?

No. I know what a real crisis is and it has
nothing to do with sitting in a hair salon staring at
my roots.

That's the part I don't like, the root issue. What
to do with the dark stuff when it comes in. How to
stay on top of the whole hair-coloring regimen.
What if I get tired of platinum hair and want to go
back to gray? Won't my friends and colleagues
react in wide-eyed astonishment, seeing my real
hair again for the first time in months, maybe
years. So what?

It's just that I'm not thrilled with the way my gray hairs stick out like barbed wire away from the younger, more supple and shiny brown hairs on my head. I thought I was beyond vanity.

But the thing is, I finally have figured out that in taking stock of what I do have, I see a path of enhancing what I see in the mirror. Gee. At this rate I might even be wearing mascara soon.

It all started the day I bought the black cashmere pajamas on sale.

It was the "50% off" sign that sucked me in the door. I've been wanting cashmere pajamas ever since I saw Katharine Hepburn wearing a pair of soft blue-and-white-piped ones in *Desk Set.* I had to do this for me. I considered the purchase carefully, feeling a hot blast of fear rise up in my throat. But that always happens when I want to spend a lot of money on myself. Suddenly I don't feel worthy, like in *Wayne's World* when Wayne and Garth meet Alice Cooper. I was taught to wear homemade clothes that didn't look as up-to-date as the other girl's fashion statements. And if you must buy new clothes, never pay full price for them.

I looked in the mirror and felt like Joan Crawford in one of her nicer film roles, when she wasn't threatening her offspring with wire hangers. How

could this be bad, to feel this good? I didn't want
to take it off. It felt too good. It felt like me.

It goes hand in hand with the hair. I thought I'd
like gray hair, relish its power to make me look like
a grown-up who has responsibility written all over
my tresses. But shit, even old people dye their hair.

Just when I think I'm beyond some cultural
norm like dyeing gray hair, I find out I'm not. Suddenly, I see that blonde hair is fun, and it's embrac-
ing a change that feels exciting and wide open. A
gutsy go-for-the-glory kind of feeling. After all, if
Emma Thompson can do it, why can't I?

Maybe instead of shaving my head, I'll just go
blonde.

First Bleached Blonde
on the Block

戣 So I went punk and didn't know it.

Wolfe bleached his hair and then dyed it blue, so I'm watching from the wings, thinking, hey, I'll be a bottle blonde—why not? It looks cool on him, so I'll try it too.

Michael starts in on my roots with powdered bleach mixed into cream developer. White globs of it fall on my bare thighs and arms. My head feels itchy but what the hell? It's only hair. If I don't like it, I'll shave it off.

I sit there like a frosted flake and after twenty minutes, Michael panics, "Go wash it off!" Emerging from the shower I see that I am now a carrot-top "blonde." The gray is gone and so is my dignity. Horrors. It's too orange. Back under the bleach for a half hour. It's less orange now but still like the sun setting through bleached hair right before it goes behind the horizon. Copper orange.

This isn't what I expected.

Wolfe bursts out laughing. Him, with his blue

hair. Mine is just bleached, for heaven's sake. Just a normal run-of-the-mill bottle blonde. So?

I uncertainly go before my first viewing audience, potential wedding clients. Not even a flicker of distaste from them. Didn't they notice that the top of my head is orange, that I look like Lucille Ball having a bad hair day? They remained calm when they saw my head without cringing and pointing. That wasn't so bad.

Soon I was venturing out into the yard for a more public viewing among neighbors who walk by my house every day. I was prickly just thinking about it. One neighbor said, "I like it."

"You do?" I asked her, like she had unbolted cranial screws.

"Yes, it's not quite lemon—it's like custard." Great. I'm balancing a dessert on my head. And her with her mother from Winston-Salem, North Carolina, standing right next to her. A mother who resembled my mother in conservative values and Bermuda shorts. She even liked it.

I was in shock.

To my other neighbor I said, "I went a little nuts." She said, "I like the orange. If it was just platinum blonde, that's more of a dumb blonde look but with the orange you look cool."

Cool, even?

And I was just getting on my bike to go get some ash-blonde dye to cover up the orange. Maybe I should just chill my jets and start enjoying the compliments. Who would have thought that someone would tell me, "It looks good?"

Well, that's a switch. My first look at myself was terror and my neighbors are being nice. But that's probably because they still want me to talk to them after I burn my hair off when I come to my senses.

And I thought I could spot a phony from across the street.

Even Michael likes it. But then he'd still like me if I weighed 300 pounds and was bald.

At first I thought, oh dear, another woman who looks desperate to get young again, as I looked at my Kool-Aid orange blonde hair and wrinkled brow. But the fact of the matter is, I'm enjoying people's mouths grazing the sidewalk in utter astonishment. Even I have to scream every time I walk by a mirror and remember, oh yeah, I'm a bottle blonde with brass highlights.

I gotta admit I was getting bored by all that lackluster gray. Why not have some fun with my head? It's just hair.

I really get why kids want to dye their hair blue or red or green. It's just playing, there's no harm in it. My generation had drugs and sex and Jimi Hendrix and bell-bottoms. They have jeans around their ankles, bald heads, red hair and bell-bottoms again. Lots of them are turning down drugs and unprotected sex.

This is just good clean fun, to dye hair blue or become a bottle blonde overnight. What the hell? It's not hurting anyone.

And I'm incognito now. No one recognizes me with sunglasses on. I'm just another bleached blonde walking down the street, wearing bike shorts and sweating, swinging one-pound hand weights and sporting a ripped T-shirt.

It's only hair.

Revelations on My 40th Year

☜ I discovered that I have my first cavity ever. I thought I was impervious to cavities but my dentist told me otherwise. Oh well. So what? I'll have my head drilled and get over it.

I realized I'm not going to be here forever. So I better get off my duff and start writing that screenplay. So I did and it still isn't done. Maybe I'll get the Oscar for original screenplay next year.

Wolfe is ten. This means that I'm ten years older than when he was born. I am now a grown-up. I can go to bed when I want to and drink vodka tonics in restaurants without the bartender asking to see my ID. I like that feeling.

I don't need my parents' permission to do anything. They wouldn't give it to me anyway. I live in California, which is impractical and shows that I ignore real estate prices like pretending I don't see a tumor growing. But I can live where I want to. I'm taller than a lot of people and therefore don't have to take anyone's shit.

I can live my live the way I want to. I'm taller, remember?

I realized I needed therapy. So now I go every two weeks to unravel just why it is that I'm so fucked up. I pay a trained professional $80 to explain it to me. And I feel that I'm getting my money's worth. She doesn't let me get away with anything. That's good.

This year I discovered that I like to work solo. I'm a big girl and can focus the camera, take my pictures and feel satisfied that I can do this on my own. I am supporting myself like I never have before. People pay me even before I do the work. For some reason they trust me. My credibility is good.

I'm taking more chances. I don't want safe anymore. It's not as fun as trying something new like filmmaking and discovering how much I love it. I took my first film class and fell in love with the Film Arts Foundation and Danny and all the people I meet there who love sitting in the dark watching movies and being in broad daylight making them. Filmmakers are fun because they manage to get their films done even without working a real job. That is inspiring.

I love Wolfe. Yesterday he told me, "Lots of people like cars for how they look, but I like cars for their luxuries." He wants a Jeep Cherokee. My landlords have "his" and "her" Cherokees. They are millionaires. Why can't I be a millionaire?

I'm beginning to realize that I can buy myself as many shoes as I want to. It's always been my dream to have about fifty pairs to choose from. Why not? I'm forty. I get to do what I want now.

I'm getting less shy about speaking up. People that know me are wrinkling their foreheads and saying she was never shy, she won't shut up ever. But that's just my close friends. I'm seeing that it's more fun to be outspoken. I never would have met Gina if I hadn't spoken up.

Gina is my newest friend that I made while being forty. I've been waiting my whole life for a friend like her. I've got to go and see her. Plan a trip together. Maybe to Calistoga or Furnace Hot Springs. She's fun and she's happy for me when I do well. Also, she is not impressed with money or status. She's beyond that. That impresses me.

I went back to North Carolina for the first time in seven years. My family acted like they just saw me yesterday. My sister went all out. She does care about me. Maybe someday she'll even listen to me. There's got to be a screenplay in it. That's it. Get to work on *Purgatory*.

Get over it! This is my mantra. Whenever the

probing needles of the world severely deflate my pincushion, I rise up and yell these three words. I no longer sit in the car with the windows rolled up doing it. This has almost entirely replaced my old mantra which was, "You stupid fuck!"

I'm planting zinnias, petunias and marigolds in my garden. And Miracle-Gro and God are giving me dinner-plate-sized dahlias.

Oh God, I'm falling asleep. It's been a big year. I need a nap.

Holes in My Head

ᕲᕳ My mouth feels like a punching bag and my tongue a wad of skin rolled up into a ball. I just had my first cavity ever drilled and filled with porcelain, the modern replacement for teeth.

I thought I had licked the cavity conspiracy. Sugar sinking into dentifrice smiles, worming its way to nerve endings—that was for other people, not me. Mary Lou, my dentist, said, "You have to do it but I don't want to be the first one to drill in your head."

I watched as they prepared for the "procedure." After wedging a block of plastic in my bite I was trussed up like a pig about to be slaughtered. They stretched this green rubber dam thing across my mouth which kept breaking, probably because I scream so much in my normal life. Then they fastened it all down with clamps and proceeded to get even more intimate. I was following them with my hand mirror as they gaily chatted about monkeys in Zaire who have sex forty-eight hours a day and do nothing else but sleep and eat. Sounds good to me.

Then, after getting their rubber dam just so,
they plunged in with gusto, cleaning and scraping
my tooth so that parts of it flew into the air above
my head. Then Mary Lou applied the needle and I
didn't even feel it after the topical anesthetic which
deadens gums like bores who dump raw sewage
on your brain. She moves in for the kill and I
swear to God I didn't feel the drilling until she hit a
"minor" nerve in my second cavity, and I flinched
off my blanketed headrest and wanted to leap
through the plate-glass window. It got better.

I looked in the hand mirror and saw a woman
being gagged and manipulated. The claustrophobia
alone is disturbing, but I like Mary Lou and I
would not want anyone else to touch my gumline
or drill out the holes in my head. She's worth the
400 bucks.

They gave me a Walkman to listen to but I
didn't want to miss any of their conversation.
Mary Lou is very good at running commentaries
meant to make responses unnecessary. And she
knows exactly what I mean when I grunt at her.
Right before she began drilling, I said, "I'm glad
you guys are doing it. And not my father."

There's something mentally unsettling about
having a father who pries out your bicuspids to
make room for your new teeth. It didn't bother me

at the time, but you really can't complain much when your father is wielding a huge needle of Novocain in the same hand that is used for spankings. Maybe that's it. Mary Lou says, "Did you tell your father about the cavity?"

No, I didn't. I just don't want to let him down.

I always thought he'd love me in a special way as long as I continued to have a mouth full of sparkly tooth enamel, devoid of fillings, which was something my brother and sisters couldn't give him. After forty years of excavating people's mouths he might be upset, and then I'll be upset and the fluoride treatments he gave me when I was ten will all be in vain. Just the thought of telling him makes me peevish and shivery. I'll tell him later on, after my mouth goes back to feeling like a mouth.

Now I'm going to lay down and recover from having my teeth jackhammered.

Sagging or Sutures?

扴 I was trying to build up my self-esteem, so I looked in the mirror and practiced saying, "Mary, I love and approve of you exactly as you are." And then I noticed for the first time ever how the skin above my eyelids cascades onto my eyelashes like an uncircumcised penis.

I haven't looked that closely at my eyes in years. Being blind and giving up mascara did it to me. I feel like one of those dogs with all the extra skin around their necks. And I didn't notice it until today. When I was supposed to be falling in love with myself.

I've been reading *How to Heal Your Life*, by Louise Hay. And for my second walk through the book I'm actually doing the exercises, not just skimming over them to get to the next part.

I have a ways to go in the self-esteem area. After looking in the mirror I see why women get their eyelids nipped and tucked. I have some compassion for them.

But it would hurt too much. Just because the skin above my eyes is rippling like ocean waves, sagging over my eyeballs, obscuring sparkly irises and soul-baring pupils, is no reason to have surgery. For me.

If only I hadn't looked that closely in the mirror, I wouldn't have known. But no, I had to try and love myself today.

Obviously this is part of my lesson. To learn to laugh at my wrinkles, gray hair and flaccid skin. That word "flaccid" is so irritating. It shouldn't be allowed in the English language.

I just didn't realize how cute I was when my skin was firm. I was too mired down in the fact that a certain boy didn't notice me, therefore I must be obese, ugly and lacking in pizzazz. His opinion was more important than my own. And he probably didn't even know I was alive either. I thought if my hair was greasy, then I must be an awful person. And if I wasn't popular, then I must be an ogre and no one would ever like me.

This was all happening when my stomach was flat, and I could eat can after can of miniraviolis, countless Almond Joys and tubs of soda without gaining an ounce. It's absurd that I chose to see myself this way, when in reality I was a slender girl with a quick mind and a sense of humor. What's not to like? So what if Peter Dwyer grew tired of me—did that mean I should sabotage my inner core with self-talk that sucks?

No-funitis seeped into my veins and I was convinced I was gross. At least until the next boy noticed me.

How embarrassing.

I could have been having fun instead of sobbing along with the Bee Gees singing "Mean Mistreator" and bemoaning the fact that Peter Dwyer no longer cared for me.

I should have just taken up acting.

So there I was, pretty and slim with toned firm skin, pert bosom and legs up to my neck, thinking I was somehow not enough. What a boob.

Now that I am digging up self-esteem from below my own floorboards, I must celebrate what I have, sags and all. How ironic.

But I don't want to be younger. I just want to steer clear of vanity and know that I am enough, finally.

Perhaps doing it without the mirror is better.

Now I know why I don't peer down on a mascara wand, flicking black fluid onto my lashes. I don't want to look that closely. I might see imperfections. That's why I never weigh myself. I don't want to know how much gravity per pound is pulling on each square inch of me. No thanks. I don't want to spend my weeknights at Weight Watchers' meetings, trying not to face my poundage. I am

enough, remember? Now that I'm older, everything is more precious. I didn't know that when I
was young. I thought I'd never die and each day
was a seamless journey of electric rollers and
laughing and flirting.

The only thing different is the rollers.

And there's a lot more now. I can appreciate
the beauty of a blossoming daffodil, the first cup of
coffee of the day, a peaceful moment in the house,
a revealed insight. And I just want to laugh more.
It washes away all the temporary problems—bills,
bullies and blustering ego.

I didn't know that before.

I was too concerned by the boys' reaction to
me. Then, when I got too much attention, I hid
behind shaggy clothes, not wanting to deal with it
all. I figured if no one knew I had shapely legs,
then I wouldn't have to deal with sexual innuen-
does. My legs were covered in khaki, my boobs
under big shirts and my heart paved over with sar-
casm and suspicion.

My pitiful slogan was, "Men are only interested
in one thing, sex."

Now, I know that yes, men are interested in
sex, and so am I. But they're not only interested in
that, unless we give our phone numbers to men
who should not have them.

When sex is sacred to us, it becomes a holy experience. After all the lovers who didn't work out, I realize that sex was a detriment. I gave in too soon to keep them interested, pretended they loved me and emphasized children after the first roll in the hay.

It didn't work.

I finally believe all those grandmothers who said, "Why buy the cow if you're getting free milk?"

Sex is just too holy to squander on the insensitive boors I used to date.

So now that I'm almost a grown-up and dating my husband full-time, I'll just get more massages. I feel younger after mine. I'm able to see that I was just tired and taut around the heart and not relaxed enough to see the truth. I'm still alive and that's a great alternative to being dead.

The answer is, get over it!

Children:
Higher Up on the
Food Chain

Preteen

Pie

Parents

Parrot fish

Plankton

Baby Born in
My Own Bedroom

༜ An advertisement in a newsletter caught my
eye. It was a six-week course in the "Achievement
of Natural Childbirth." Achievement? When I tell
people that my one and only child was born at
home, their eyebrows arch into their hairlines and
they assume I'm operating on too few cylinders.
They don't act like I've achieved anything, except
for maybe a cameo role on *Little House on the
Prairie.*

Here's the real story. I didn't want starchy-faced
people in white coats pricking—they call it "tap-
ping"—my spine with a huge needle to make me
"relax" for labor. That's why they call it labor;
there is actual work involved. The hardest work
that can ever be done—passing a football through
a hole the size of a swizzle stick.

I wanted the atmosphere to be serene so I
would feel comfortable screaming like a samurai. I
hoped to have my water break within the comfort
of my own kitchen and not have to drive anywhere

just to be hooked up to some fetal monitor and be told that it was taking too long, so it's time for a C-section. If it's longer than five hours the doctors act like you really should have called ahead and reserved a time slot with them because they have to go to Pebble Beach and golf right now.

June, my midwife, arrived mid-afternoon fresh from a family outing. She covered up all the clocks with infant-sized Pampers so I'd forget how long this was taking and settled in with us for way over twelve hours. Please write and tell me if you know of any doctor living today who would stand by a woman in labor, calmly sipping coffee, singing to her, making her laugh and providing emotional guardrails on the slippery slope of birthing a baby on this planet. I don't know any, either. But June was there to welcome me into motherhood, still perky after hours of angst and ready to crack jokes. You don't get that kind of treatment at Stanford Hospital.

She makes light of her contribution and gives me all the accolades. I like that in a midwife. Guys seem to think they can help you to breathe during labor. I wanted to breathe, all right. Like a dragon snorting fire.

Guys, please remember this when you tell us to "breathe with the contraction." Breathe shmeathe,

it hurts like being turned inside out and having
your pelvis torn apart at the roots—don't tell me to
practice my Lamaze, when the only work you did
was putting Mr. Hard-on inside me. We can't really
call that work, now can we?

Natural childbirth sounds like a woman slipping
sylphlike over a meadow in silken raiment, softly
blowing in the breeze. But that isn't what
happened to me. Here's what did:

∽ I yelled louder than any human being alive and
   wondered why my neighbors on the other side
   of the wall didn't beat down my door in
   protest.

∽ I gained a healthy respect for the act of getting
   pregnant. This is serious and it may be a
   joyous romp in the hay for you menfolk, but for
   we women it's nine months of assorted
   degrees of puking, heartburn, back pain,
   waddling and the best—being treated like a
   holy relic in public because damn it, I am.

∽ I achieved more belligerence toward stupidity
   and psychotic in-laws.

After pushing my son out of my body I felt a
non-drug-induced high of realization that after pro-
ducing a whole human being, anything else is

easy, you know, like directing a movie, writing a book, being authentic. I just had to quit whining and get off my duff, just like during labor.

I had the best bath of my life after Wolfe was born. I soaked in an herb-infused broth designed to tighten up my sagging yoni and tired skin with magic herbs from June's black bag.

I achieved an absolute respect for every woman walking down the street who shared this incredible, eye-and-innards-opening experience with me. I found myself thinking, if men were the ones to bear children they'd demand we put them on thrones and run to get their beers, but women act all modest about growing a human being inside us. During labor we hang on to our root hairs, our thread to reality, our last bit of humor, our strength we didn't know we had, our incredulity that this is what we have to do and that we cannot take a nap like our husbands can right now.

I achieved widespread gigantic hints of my own chromosomal damage for choosing to trust my soul, body and baby to God and stay home, far from fetal monitors and self-important male doctors explaining how to relax with the contraction, when they'll never feel one. A friend advised me, "You are going to have a back-up unit with medical equipment in your driveway, aren't you?"

I got a gorgeous baby boy. A perfectly perfect
boy who was born with a Palm Springs tan and a
powerful urge to suck and tell me exactly how he
felt about absolutely everything—without English
words.

It was enormously peaceful and satisfying to
climb into my own bed, the bed where Wolfe was
conceived, after he wriggled his way out from
between my legs and demanded to be heard. I
didn't have to try sleeping in a ward of nursing
mothers attended by overzealous chattering relatives. I didn't have to ring for my baby to be
brought to my bedside after being poked and
prodded and measured and syringed, all cleaned
up for public perusal.

It was too heady of an experience to walk on
two legs so I crawled on all fours when I couldn't
stand up after my bath, inching my way to the bed
and laughing. I would not be allowed to do that
through the corridors of Stanford Hospital, dodging
the racing gurneys.

Okay. I get it. I did achieve natural childbirth.
It's a high you don't get with Pitocin. It was so natural. I didn't want to take drugs; I thought I'd miss
something.

I was all there, even parts of me that wanted to
take a nap and make Michael do the rest of it. He

got off easy and stole my spotlight by serenading others with his tired old story, "I had a dream about how to hold Mary while she was in labor. . . ." So? I had to push the kid out and spill my placenta on the bedroom floor and then step in it with my bare foot.

Okay. So I'm angry. It only happened ten years ago. Ten years ago on February 9 we reached into heaven and pulled out a child. A baby, fresh and sweet from divinity. And now, ten years later, we'll be hosting an overnight party for six rambunctious, ten-year-old prepubescent boys. How did this happen?

Our dimpled-wrist baby grew up and now demands that he and his cohorts receive twenty-four hours of room service and nonstop Nintendo entertainment. I draw the line at the rental of a blow-up enclosed trampoline in the driveway.

I do have my standards.

I have achieved steering a child from conception to pregnancy to near puberty and that is an achievement, bigger than all you CEOs out there of blue-chip companies. Just try and see how strong you are after pushing a baby's head through an opening the size of a soda straw. Just try it. This just might give you more humility towards every woman on earth who has asked for a baby and actually got one.

It ain't no boardroom; it's dancing with angels and going past, way past any threshold of pain to a room that opens up huge after crawling on all fours through a tunnel the size of an earthworm.

That's what natural childbirth is. It's the most difficult thing you ever thought of being part of and also the most spiritually rewarding.

That is an achievement. The biggest thing I ever did.

Sex After Spit-up

꙰ You married a man once. Way back before the baby arrived. You'd like to talk to him sometime. But you want to take a nap or even a shower for the unfamiliar thrill of it all. You look at your lover. He is basking in breast milk spit-up and wondering how to pay the rent this month.

It's been a few weeks since the baby, your baby, has arrived. You know that the husband is interested in sex. With you, even. But you can't imagine anything that large entering your body rather than exiting it. Having just given birth to a football you are stretched out and enlarged like the Grand Canyon. The husband will just have to live with the new size of your own personal Idaho.

The thought of having anyone, even the man you have decided to spend the rest of your Christmases with and the person whose relatives you are forced to entertain, lying on your overhandled skin makes you nauseous. You're still clammy from cuddling the baby all day. And now you're supposed to promenade in crotchless panties, putting on a performance. The poor man is drooling for affection and you feel like a used washcloth.

Your idea of ecstasy is to sit in hot water, locking the door behind you and barricading it with police tape.

You're wondering if you'll ever have sex again, knowing that the baby will cry and you'll jump up like a private in boot camp responding to a drill sergeant. You simply can't imagine ever relaxing again. It might be hormonal. That's what the men in white coats call it. But then, they've never had to push a baby out the smallest opening in their bodies, either. It's a little deeper than just estrogen.

No matter what kind of labor you had, and spare me the descriptions of two-hour deliveries full of chanting and smiling, you are exhausted.

No one told you about the leaking lochia seeping out of your underwear whenever you sit down. The bits and pieces of afterbirth fluid that are expressed just as you're entertaining the mother-in-law's first peek at the baby. It's wise to just sit on one of those hospital mats without undies and give up on decorum. Then all the lochia can collect in one place and you won't be leaving deposits all over the house. People don't tell you about this because they are embarrassed. I, however, care about you and want you to avoid staining your best chairs.

The subject of lochia is too often neglected in the postpartum textbooks. Sitting without panties will limit your circle of acquaintances and friends, who must have a look at the baby and see how you fared through the ordeal. But who needs to be popular when you're leaking from every orifice and entertaining crowds at the same time, who dismiss you as soon as they lay eyes on the baby?

Then the inane questions will begin. Are his eyes open yet? Like he's some kind of newborn ostrich or hamster. Can he hear anything? For some reason people assume they are looking at a freshly fertilized zygote that happened to pop out of incubation before falling asleep again.

Does he sleep through the night yet? And this after two days of being a citizen of our planet. Geez! Of course, he will never sleep through the night! I don't sleep through the night ten years later. I'm in training for when he starts driving in six years and I have to wait for the sound of his engine arriving in the driveway.

Who does he look like? I just had a fully formed human being come out of my body and now I have to entertain opinions from the assembled guests on whom he is the carbon copy of. Really, I don't care if he has my eyes and Michael's mouth. I just want him to support me in the manner to

which I've become accustomed when I hit the age
of 100 and want to retire. I produced a miracle and
the peanut gallery wants to analyze his facial
features rather than see him as his own uncatego-
rized amazing self.

All right, so he is a lot more handsome than
Brad Pitt.

Someday, after you've had enough naps and
the relatives have scattered, taking their promises
to baby-sit with them, you will want to have sex
again. Maybe even wear a short skirt to entice
your loverman. The guy you married, remember?
But having sex now, when you stay up all night
breastfeeding and shuffle around in slippers by day
while entertaining thoughts of a bath, just doesn't
compute.

You wonder how it is that babies are created
from this one act of sex and then become your
lifelong responsibility. Rolling around in the hay or
the woods or the beach, or wherever it was that
you consummated and conceived, is a far cry
from shouldering breasts the size of Montana and
sleepwalking through life, watching the house start
to look like tumbleweeds skittering across the dust
bowl.

What you have to do is delegate. If you don't
get help you might be convinced never to have sex

again, or to just run away from home and live quite comfortably in the Pyrenees, wearing a hair shirt for the rest of your life just so you can get an uninterrupted night's sleep.

Beg your friends to help you, even if you have to bribe them. You will. What you really need is a full-time nursemaid and a secretary and a cook. But you still might require the help of an anesthesiologist. It's nice to receive little outfits with words like "slugger" and a baseball bat sewn on them, but what you really need is a two-hour nap. Do anything you can to be able to sleep during the day when the sun is streaming through the windows and you think you have to clean out the toilet bowl. Resist any thoughts of domesticity. Head straight for your bed and lie down.

After about six months you might feel like sex again.

Infancy and In-laws

৬ Take in-laws. Yes, you can have mine. Laying down the rules with in-laws is necessary for a healthy functioning mind and marriage. You mainly just want to limit the unasked-for advice. Here are the rules.

1. Give me a break. I'll never be on time again. And I'm so sorry I didn't get to call you back. I was breastfeeding for twelve hours straight.

2. We don't want to know your secrets of raising a child because you really blew it raising the one I'm married to. He has divulged painful stuff that you couldn't possibly remember because you were off to Europe, shopping for new clothes and jewelry.

3. You are not going to let your child spend his entire childhood crying from neglect. It doesn't spoil the baby to pick him up when he cries.

4. When the in-laws are serving their dinner at 9 PM and you are passing your newborn back and forth over the gravy boat while trying to be interested in what they are saying, stop acting like a pawn and remember that you are a par-

ent now. You must mention the fact that nine o'clock works for their stomachs but you haven't digested any food since you visited them, and then get up and leave the table.

They have lost touch with the fact that about a million years ago they were babies too. Babies are not convenient but in-laws expect them to be cute at preselected hours of the day just for them. Just ask your mother-in-law not to pinch the baby's feet to wake him up for her five-minute visit.

5. The in-laws' main job is to make a fuss and bring you casseroles.

I know it can be uncomfortable to lay down the rules to your meddling in-laws but teethmarks in your tongue are painful. Just unclench your fists and begin to realize that you are not shaped like a doormat. Remind yourself that you are the only authority residing in your brain casing. Now that you are a parent you are a member of a special club called the "I Am Totally Responsible for the Well-Being of Another Human Being" club. You have more on your mind than listening to some shallow-as-a-birdbath report on how you can improve your child rearing skills.

The truth is, until your kid starts talking, you

have no idea how much you may have fucked them up. Or your amazing mothering skills may have produced an astoundingly witty child who has far surpassed you in intellect and physical prowess and spiritual acumen. You just never know.

Last night I was watching the Oscars with Wolfe and Quentin Tarantino was being interviewed on the movie-star tarmac going into the Pavilion. Wolfe says, "All the stars have bodyguards. Why are they talking to a bodyguard?" That was his take on the recipient of the Oscar for best screenplay.

This makes him wittier than I am. He is also more fun than anyone I know to watch the Academy Awards with. Your children will surprise you. Give your ego a break and open up to their fresh insight. They'll be ruling the world while we're relaxing in our rockers and sipping lemonade, so listen up. They'll be in charge someday.

Yes. It's hard to accept wisdom from someone who does not yet reach your navel. So what? It's humbling to realize that you should probably just walk around on your knees all the time without bothering to get up. You'll be doing plenty of praying when you have kids, so get used to the position. While you're down on all fours, look around you. It's good to notice where the electrical outlets are so you'll know where to look when the knives are missing from the silverware drawer.

Now is the time to redecorate your house in an early playpen theme. Put the knickknacks away and delete the word "no" from your tape loop of responses to the baby's every exploration. Tiny tots will sooner pick up a plugged-in toaster to take apart than a predictable Fisher-Price toy.

Whatever you buy them will end up ignored and covered with dust within seconds of opening the box it came in. You will long for a life without stuffed animals staring at you. You will fondly remember the days when you owned carpets. Rugs are just stain magnets that should be rolled up and left unopened right after you get them professionally cleaned.

Insist that the in-laws remove any offensively barbed jewelry at the door. Babies like to rip necklaces off necks and chew on the beads of the overendowed. Pearls are difficult to remove from your child's small intestine.

One of the best advantages to having a new baby is discarding all the worthless distractions we commit ourselves to. All of a sudden you have no time to listen while relatives drone on about their shattered lives. They will be dying to give you detailed descriptions of the architecture of their last marital dispute, but now you have rock-hard breasts that are beginning to drip and the dishes are piled high enough to reach another galaxy and you aren't out of your bathrobe yet and your lover wants to have sex since the baby fell asleep on your nipple.

In short, you have a life.

Pick off the nuisances like fuzz pilling on your favorite sweater. Don't take these phone calls from hell; just get voicemail and stay centered in your own pool of spit-up.

Unasked-for advice is always given by those who haven't had a baby in thirty years and are operating under the assumption that the diaper service comes in to change the baby when he needs his drawers cleaned out. These people are asking to have their numbers permanently forgotten.

There are many other sources of wisdom more suited to your needs than worn-out tales from the '50s warmed up to create a modern-day *Donna Reed Show*. This is the '90s and no one wears shirtwaist dresses with chokers of pearls to dust anymore.

So sledgehammer your high heels and put your dogs up. Being a mother is a forty-eight-hour-a-day job that never ends. Tell the in-laws to take a chill pill.

Someday you will be able to have a conversation with a person who won't pee on you.

Arteriosclerosis of the Mind

꧁ Wolfe went back to being "an only child" after his friend Mikey left. I immediately started feeling guilty that I hadn't provided him with a younger brother or sister to pester right now. He was kicking leaves on the sidewalk across the street, hands jammed in his jeans, a sullen look on his face.

His best friend moved to Colorado and he still hasn't found a replacement. So he doesn't have a special friend that he calls every day and plays with all the time. His closest friends are torn in two by their divorced parents so he doesn't get to see them much. The look on his face is so lonely. It's times like these that I feel selfish for "only" having one kid. Or is that just my Catholic upbringing?

Catholicism taught me that it was wise to spurt out many fully formed children so they too could praise God and partake of the Holy Eucharist and become paying contributors to the Church.

I offered to do "something" with him, oh say, read him a book, play with clay—an activity I wanted to do. He slumped in the lawn chair on the porch, suggested a bike ride, then vetoed it. "I'm too tired."

"Let's go to the creek."

"Okay."

He wasn't expecting that response. I mean, I was disinclined to get my carcass off the chair and here I was agreeing to the treachery of sliding down the banks of our backyard creek. We decided to take Fluffy too. We investigated the descent from the end of Cowper Saint, one hundred steps away from our front door. It was steep but do-able. Yeah right.

Pitched straight down to hell, I surveyed the slippery slope of my own misgivings. Oh, what the heck, I'll dive for it—what could go wrong? My adventurous spirit glowing like a kid's, I plunged in with abandon. Halfway down, the hill got steeper than I had seen from the top. My butt slipping on the dirt, my feet in zoris clinging to a loosely eroded cliff, I started picking up speed, sideswiping poison oak on my way down to the rocks below. I started praying and braying. Even Wolfe was concerned to see me about to crash-land in the creek bed. "Are you all right, Mama?"

In my short skirt, my new $25 Irish undies scraping the last bit of rock face, I was not all right but I did discover a root with my big toe and clung to it like a woman who has been jilted and keeps thinking the lover will return. Then God stepped in. Thank you, God, because I didn't want to road burn my ass and land with a splash and a few broken bones into rubble below. I was to be saved!

"I'm sorry, Mom."

Too bad I don't have the body of a nine-year-old anymore. Just what the hell was I thinking, believing I'm not in the full bloom of middle age? Those words "middle age" are so creepy. I had to defy those words by descending into the creek bed. I just didn't tell my knees about it. Or they weren't listening. But I had to do it.

"We don't have to go back, do we?" The poor guy was expecting a volley of midlife complaining and bellowing about crises and crash landings. But no. "Isn't it nice down here?" he hopefully inquired.

Yes, it was. The sun had sunk low in the trees bordering the creek, casting soft light on the water as it sparkled in the curves of the creek bed that undulated into the limelight of a magnificent sunset. I was enchanted. I immediately thought, why don't we come down here more often? It's steps from our front porch, a living and breathing creek and my creaky attitude keeps me out of it

because I might have to change my thinking for a
minute. I started to relax. Wolfe was all lit up,
skipping stones expertly onto the surface of the
stream.

"Will you teach me how to do it?" I asked.

He jumped to the challenge and showed me in
slow-motion detail exactly how the flat stone
leaves the fingertips of your hand and goes skid-
ding across the water.

I screamed in glee when I got my first one. He
looked like a proud parent. I was so thrilled I did it
finally. And in my own backyard too. I started
making plans for "beach" trips down here, away
from my sequestered thinking up above. We skip-
ped stones, meandered to the other side of the
stream, Fluffy barking at us to come back, found
oddly shaped stones and discussed friendship and
climbing up the concrete bags rather than the dirt
hill to get out.

"One slip and you'd die, Mama."

It takes a nine-year-old to tell me that. I thought
it was a good idea to climb up the concrete cliff
that discouraged erosion into the creek bed. The
kid was right; thank God I brought him.

In the middle of a city, at the placid hour of
sunset, I felt sweetly protected by softly flowing
water and emerald green oak and alder trees,

muffling traffic and the teeming urgency of commuters returning from work on a Friday.

I found peace in the creek. And I was such a sludge about going down there, past the poison oak.

I felt closer to Wolfe. He said abashedly, "Oh God, my only friend is my mother."

Well, it's a good place to start.

Next time I'll bring a rope.

Veal Chops versus Tofu Pups

৩ We're getting more furtive around here about eating meat in front of that nougat-filled divinity boy of ours. That's why I spent $58 on lobster tails today when no one was looking. It's seafood, not meat. That explanation fails to satisfy our preteen of pure living.

He discovers we are eating crab legs again and he disgustedly yells, "What's that smell?" as if a ton of rotten eggs had been deposited on his bed and we failed to notice. He decides to eat under the kitchen table while he berates us for killing animals.

"But lobsters and crabs are ugly," I weakly counter.

"So, just 'cuz it's ugly it deserves to die?" He has a point there.

"But what about chickens—they're disgusting. And cows have zero personality." I'm really reaching here.

"Mom, how many cows had to die for your couch, four of them?" he says with utter disdain.

Why did I have to get such a conscious child?
Well, I suppose it is good. I have cut back on
the meat entrées. I'm tired of him eating under
the table.

The kid's trying to convert us from heathen
status to Zen Buddhism.

It all started when we insisted upon yearly
vacations at our favorite Zen monastery—Tassajara
in Carmel Valley, far from phones and glamour.

While we drank scotch in our room and listened
to the creek babble, Wolfe joined the Zen students
in their kitchen, preparing meals that threaten to
topple Greens restaurant's reputation and fame. He
sliced, diced and washed lettuce on a step stool to
reach the counter. He wisecracked along with the
best of them and we were fondly looked upon as
"Wolfe's parents." He was the celebrity; we were
the chauffeurs. The Zen students smiled at us just
for being parents. It was more acknowledgment
than we got from our own families.

We decided to keep coming back year after
year. After five or six days of meatless meals even
I begin to believe it's unnecessary cruelty. But then
I eat some fried chicken and change my mind.
But that barbecued tofu they made us was
heavenly. How come my vegetarian cooking falls
short of theirs?

It takes more time to be pure. That's the reason.
I'm enamored of throwing chicken in the oven to
bake, mixing up a salad and calling it a meal. This
takes fifteen minutes, tops. To barbecue tofu I have
to plan ahead and maybe even give up my cocktail hour. I have to be present for every step of the
meal preparation so that I don't cut off my pointer
finger in a zealous flurry of chopping onions and
garlic.

In other words, I have to work.

"Why do we always have meat on the holidays?"
Wolfe questions us.

"Well . . . we're celebrating."

"Yeah, we're celebrating death!"

Okay, okay. I thought instead of the usual
Christmas beef tenderloin that practically cooks
itself, I'll capitulate by serving up lobster tails that I
can hide in a bed of Boston lettuce on the plate.
Wolfe likes to place large crockery bowls and
cereal boxes between our plates and his so he
doesn't have to view the carnage.

He is not amused when we order whole baked
flounder at our favorite Chinese restaurant and it
comes to the table with its head still on, eyes staring vacantly at the other diners. Lying in a pool of
chili sauce, it looks like it was recently clubbed and
snatched from its watery home. We start to drool

and Wolfe dives under the table, saying, "I'm not coming up until it's gone."

To make matters worse all our best friends are vegetarian too. But they tolerate meat-eaters with better humor, even sleep with them. He has a phalanx of our nearest and dearest who silently support him every time he refuses chicken and Burger King.

Well, why don't we get with the program?

I was once a vegetarian and liked it just fine. Then Michael moved into my life and asked for a lamb roast, reminding me that barbecued T-bones do taste delicious. Especially with herbed butter melting on top. I slowly stopped shopping at the Real Foods Co-op and nibbled heavily at my cooking job in a restaurant that heralded veal chops and bluefish. So what to eat for a snack? I grazed among the grilled salmon, industrial-sized Häagen-Dazs tubs and freely roamed in the walk-in cooler, sampling prawns and puffed pastry wrapped around chicken breasts. I started to get a gut. Ten pounds later I advanced to the next larger size in standard-issue chef pants. I told myself, this is just from tasting the food.

So I was back on meat, fatter and less inclined to exercise. Did I take on the personality of a penned-in cow or what? Does eating meat do that to you? Make you sluggish and unmotivated? Those aren't words I'd ever use to describe Mr. Zen-priest-in-training.

I didn't have midriff bulge when I refrained from eating meat. I felt lighter and more ethereal. Or was that just being twenty-two years old?

The less emphasis on food the better. I feel much better when a handful of nuts suffices or a salad quenches my starvation. Weighed down by animal matter I see the difference in my gait and attitude and lust for living.

Okay, so there's been far too much indulging around here. Chocolate every hour, incoming gift sweets, lobster tails on Christmas, smoked salmon and cream cheese on bagels for breakfast—what next? I silently repeat my mantra, "It's the holidays" and take another sip of wine.

After New Year's I'll swim more and eat less prime rib. I'll be more outgoing and upbeat. I will play more and stop whining. Eat more roughage and grains. Less Hawaiian chips and sour cream dip.

I'll be more like my kid and less like an adult. I'll eat more spinach and less fat-infused chicken.

"Teach your parents well" is what it amounts to.

Being a Mother
Wearing Blinders

೧೨ The phone bellows, the fax blurts and the mail belches. I remain in my seat, calmly oblivious. I do not move a muscle. I am rooted to this cushion. If I get up I'll just continue with what is required of me, making money and returning phone calls and hanging wash.

I'm a writer so I sit here and write. I am seeking solace in this thin computer, far from the typhoon of my regular life.

George Lucas and Woody Allen don't answer their phones either. I always thought it odd that Woody did this but now I know why. Blocking out all the noise, forging ahead with my spirit in full sail is the prescription for connecting with the divine. It has nothing to do with voicemail and sifting through junk papers.

All of a sudden this morning, when I tried to nail a board back to the fence and realized it was a job for a skilled carpenter, I wanted to start writing immediately and forget this handyman facade I had going. I have no business fixing a fence that requires more artistry than I'm going to give it. It was a slapdash job and I knew it but at least the fence won't cave in today. Maybe tomorrow it'll cave in, but not today.

I've been gone for three days and life as I know it has been walking on beaches, snooping around a castle and sitting in the ocean breeze and hiking through cypresses so thick we were on our hands and knees crawling under branches. This is how normal life should be, but I don't have an assistant to attend to mundane chores like returning phone calls and masterminding my calendar, arranging appointments for me. Oh, and by the way, cooking all my meals and attending to my fine washables and cleaning out the basement and sending off samples of my writing to publishers and showing my photography at galleries.

Just a few things like that so I can continue my studies of cultivating cacti and inspecting insects burrowing in pine needles and writing screenplays. And being a full-time mother instead of a halfback mother who bellows commands from the kitchen and has half-baked responses to my son's keen and observant commentary because he was supposed to be in bed two hours ago and he wants a light snack before retiring, but only after this story

and then you can make me a melted cheese sandwich, Mom.

See, I just don't have it together. My child does
not respond to my requests to put on his shoes for
the 400th time. Instead, he goes to his room and
starts looking for a CD to put on while he ties his
shoes and then decides that his dresser, which is
now an official archeological dig, needs sifting
because he just found his pocketknife which has
been missing for months and there might be other
treasures up there that he hasn't seen in years.

This morning he was irate.

"Why can't I go to a wedding with you?"

I go to weddings to find myself behind a camera and anticipate magical moments happening
while I wait in the wings of God's robe, watching.
I am quiet and focused. It does not go with being
a parent.

The last time he went to a wedding with me his
tooth fell out just as I was taking portraits of the
bride before she got married. He ran up to me
with his gumline bleeding and a stump of tooth in
his hand. While he dripped blood I had to take pictures of the bride. I felt like a misaligned turnip.
Brain-dead and suffering from my own ignorance
of the important things in life. But I had just driven
four hours on a crooked road to get to this wed-

ding and now I had to earn my $2000. Even if teeth are falling from gumlines and he'll never be this age again. I felt like a heel that's been ground down to a nub and is wearing into the shoe leather. I vowed to never take him to a wedding again. He might need me to be a mother again.

I go to work to have fun and be with brides and grooms falling in love with each other right in front of me. They don't yell at me or even demand special treatment. They don't ask for cooked-to-order meals, rides to friends' houses right now or money on the spur of the moment. They do not run up to me with catalogs in their hands, eyes ablaze, demanding this unusual deck of cards that sings or that small motor vehicle that drives itself around a city block and barely notices that you aren't even in it. I go to work to forget that I'm a maid at home.

"You don't like me, do you?" he asked.

Then I felt like a heel even worse than before. Like a churlish, jaded, no-fun, dried-out shell of a human being who needs an infusion of fresh air and a new attitude. "Tude," as it is called nowadays. My tude sucks. "Okay," I told him, "I'll pay you $2 to get me ready for a wedding."

"Two dollars!" he bellows. "I need $50 to buy a new game and I can make $20 very easily." I tried to explain to him that needing money and what the market will bear are two very different concepts. He stopped listening after I opened my mouth. His ears closed up and I wasn't feeling energetic enough to chip through the concrete with a jackhammer. Besides, his backpack was missing and he was going to be late for school.

Sometimes his deepest revelations are delivered from inside our frantic pace to get him to school or to bed, and I don't hear his insight all the way through. That's when I need to slow down and remember that being a mother is about being a Zen priest, but harder. Shedding the sense of time and feeling the beauty in his questions now, before he grows up and drives away with the keys to my car. He's already ten. And he's not only gaining on me, he's surpassed me. He's wittier, more direct and swears less than I do. He regards me from behind his new hip sunglasses and knows I'm hopelessly behind the times. I can tell by the arch of his eyebrows. He wishes I'd get a clue but knows I'll just get by.

But he still kisses me in public so I'm happy. It's far better than drinking doubles on a weekend night.

Now if I could just get with the program and learn how to differentiate his pop groups from one another. I don't know the Dead Presidents from the Presidents of the United States and the current dictators in office now.

I have so much to learn and an exasperated child to teach me.

Getting Out of Dodge

ॐ I was dying to leave town but I had no idea it would be with eighty-seven fourth graders. I burned rubber leaving the curb while my neighbor, an eighty-year-old woman whose full-time job is gossip, was watching; she was sure that I was leaving Michael. She was disappointed when she found out that it was just a three-day field trip with a passel of preteens in the foothills of the Sierras on the south fork of the American River.

I had to go. I was at school earlier in the day, saying good-bye to the kids on the bus and they kept asking me to go with them. It's hard to ignore a bevy of boisterous ten-year-old girls, saying, "Please come with us," irrational sincerity and love emblazoned across their pure faces. Then I discovered that my camera bag was on the bus with all the sleeping bags, heading up to the river without me. With my car keys in it.

The principal drove me home. She was on her way up there to be with the kids. It was another nudge. So I gave up my quiet house, my work, Fluffy, horny dates at restaurants, listening to myself think and time alone. My heart was tugging

me toward the American River, where I realized I
surely must have a screw loose to dash up there
without a sleeping bag or a pillow.

What was I thinking?

When I arrived, Susan, the fourth grade
teacher, said, "I love you!" Well. I'm a sucker for
love and I was getting it in spade-fulls. Wolfe was
in shock that I was in the flesh and wanted to
know, "Why are you here?"

I said, "You forgot your toothbrush, so here I
am."

It's sort of like prison. Lynn, the camp director,
stopped me on the way to my room. "Why are
you up here?" she asks with a furrowed brow. I
answered with an edge in my voice, "I came up to
get a cookie."

Oh geez. I imagined flying on rope swings
across the American River, yelling like banshees.
Oh well. We have to keep the little critters alive.
We don't want them washed down the river so we
must stay bolted to their bodies at all times, and if
anyone so much as touches the river they get
boxed and sent back home UPS ground.

I'm having fun with the girls. Ten-year-old girls
are very concerned with their hair, boys, their hair
and boys. And they can mimic their teachers perfectly, which sends me into spasms. These kids kill

me with their wit. The girls excitedly discuss who likes whom and which boys are the current favorites. I told them, "Teddy's cute," and they said, "But he's so obnoxious," in a disdainful tone. The hormones are racing, zinging through the air, sparking bush-fires. Whoa.

For some reason they like me because I say yes to everything and I eat the food off their plates so they don't get in trouble for "wasting." It's a giant slumber party with girlfriends who line up to get their hair French braided.

I'd love a shot of whiskey but booze and fire-arms aren't allowed. Maybe tomorrow night when things loosen up a bit.

The authorities have told me, in five words or less, what it means to be a camp counselor. I'm glad I didn't go to the parent training meetings before the trip because all the fun would have been sucked out of this. As it is, I have to be a drill sergeant who can put thirty girls to bed and insist on their total acceptance of my much higher position on the food chain. Instead, I agree to ask their favorite boys which girls they like and then report back with the answers. I break rules every day, like suggesting that they remove their bathing suits to take a shower and throwing out food that was supposed to be weighed after every meal to determine how much waste was being generated by their overeager response to what was offered. After three days it was only eighteen pounds. That's how much my poodle weighs.

I learned how to discourage kids from whining after almost slitting my wrists on a five-mile hike, hearing two kids out of eleven complain about the heat, the hike, the lack of water and the boredom. Oh sure, their parents were off having spa treatments while I had to monitor their kids' behavior on top of a sweaty hill, watching them fight with one another, wearing tundra coats in 80-degree weather.

Kasi told me, "They have a secret handshake. They bang their heads against poles." I did not make this up. She also told me, "John memorized his license plate and has been singing a song about it for a whole year."

So here's what you say to children that you can't stand anymore: "Go to your room because I can't teach you anything right now. When your mouth is saying those words, your mind is closed, and you can't learn anything when your mind is closed." How true.

It didn't work on the five-mile hike, though.

I love being outside. I learn more from this than hanging around bores who won't shut up. A river

I'll listen to, but not overfed experts who believe
there's nothing new they can learn. The teachers
are so patient. I say, get over it if a kid fails to see
the six-inch iron beam in his face and whacks his
head on it.

I'm a little rough around the edges. I learned a
lot by opening my nailed-shut mind and allowing it
to breathe. Michael said, "You look all aired-out"
when I returned home after my wilderness experience. It's true. I wanted to stay another day, braving the night in an airless room with the windows
nailed shut.

All these things don't matter when you're having a good time and are so exhausted that nothing
matters, only the sound of the river rushing by. I
was the last to fall asleep at night and the first to
get up every morning.

At night I sat listening to the American River
and rejoiced in the fact that I could hear its thunder
and felt moved by the power coursing under me.
My petty complaints washed away down the shore.
I was falling in love with the place. Even with all
the rules. I sat there in the black velvet air wondering when I'd be back to ride a rubber flotation
device down the rapids. Rooted on that wooden
chair my brain cells woke up my soul, saying, you
gotta get out more in the divinity of nature!

A walk at the shopping mall pales in comparison. Purchasing new shoes made in another country, far from the soles of my feet, is shallow compared to hiking through oak trees and feeling the wind whip up from the river into my face, hearing the rapids churn and spill by in a fury of unstoppable purpose and power. Why can't I be like that?

The answer is, I can be.

My eyes started to close. It was time to go to bed and get ready to leave the next day. I was sad that it was almost over. I liked hanging with ten-year-old girls, listening to their troubles, reflections, fights and opinions. They are articulate, sober, hilarious, deep, positive, and utterly unstoppable—like the river.

The next day:

The coffee sucks, the kids are whining and I'm having a great time. I love how a river doesn't negotiate. It just flows around the boulders and keeps going. Attitude is everything.

I tried to convince myself of that last night each time I woke up, tossing like Caesar salad on a makeshift pillow, a blanket wrapped around a thin pad of foam, who knows where it's been before. But I like my grown-up bunkmate, who told me her husband died of a brain tumor and she thought it

was just his sinuses. When he started going blind
she said, "It's just stress." I would have done
exactly the same thing. I'm forever pooh-poohing
Michael's ailments. It gave me a start to find out
her husband keeled over, kicked the bucket and
permanently left town, all at the age of thirty-
seven. She's one hip chick, carrying on valiantly
herself with two kids.

A male parent on the trip asked me today,
"You have just the one?" Just because he has three
kids. I said, "There's nothing 'just' about it." Women
have to force a kid out of a hole less than the
diameter of a dime, while men contribute the
sperm. If Michael ever brings up the story about
how Wolfe was born and I didn't have anything to
do with it, frying pans will fly.

I thought about the flask of scotch in my baggage. It remained unopened. The river was intoxicating enough. What a liquor that is. Besides, I
made up for it last night. Michael took me to a
white-tablecloth restaurant and we kept talking for
hours about our three-day separation, which was
good for our marriage. It was the best sex I've had
in a long time.

It was fun to be at boot camp, bitching about
the rules and the next day falling in love with the
night air and the oak trees and the river and the

camaraderie. We four womenfolk juggled thirty girls between us and did it with grace and wisdom. Well, they did, anyway. I was breaking rules with the kids and talking about staying up late and whispering together.

The last morning was the best. After a walk by the river I sat on Cathy's bed. Cathy's my neighbor who I have never bothered to get to know, preferring instead to believe that I was invisible to her and finding out that I really liked her and we made each other laugh too. We sat there with five girls, luxuriating in the no cooking and no carpools and no one to take care of other than thirty girls who liked us and opened our minds a crack with their unbridled joy and tenacity.

Ginny, another co-counselor, is a surgical nurse! She told me how the doctor she was performing open heart surgery with said, "There's an unusual amount of blood pooling at my feet. Someone find out where it's coming from." That's what she deals with on a daily basis. And she also has three kids who are far from sedentary. She juggles it all.

I was clearly the only flake in the bunch. But no. There was a reason I was there. It was to listen to the river and laugh with ten-year-old girls who told me, "You're like a kid." I take that as a compliment.

I have to be a parent to Wolfe, but I can be more
of an Auntie Mame with them.

So we all let down our hair and got comfy with
one another. You have to be when you haven't had
any coffee and your hair is standing up in towers
above your head because you slept on it wet. And
you walk in on a fellow roommate in the bathroom
buttoning up their pants. It was better than summer camp because I'm now old enough to be a
counselor.

On the last night I read the counselor rule book,
just for fun, and found out that I was not a paragon
of adulthood to the girls when I suggested that I'd
be happy to find out which boys liked them. I did
not administer or threaten any "checks" for misbe-
havior. And I instigated noncompliance with the
rules when I told them that I would not put my
fingers in the air in a peace sign to get them to be
quiet like all the other parents. I would ask them to
be quiet and that would be that. It only worked
once. But I did have fun and I'm going to remember this episode for the rest of my life. I can hear
the girls' voices ringing in my head: "You're so
fun!" "Oh goodie! You're our counselor!" Hey, I'm a
sucker for total acceptance.

I don't get that in my family. I have a long list
of felonies after my name, according to the people

I live with. Like swearing and being pissed off and not doing what they want me to and other infractions that carry even more weight. But damn it, I was treated like a goddess for whole minutes at a time and I loved it. And I got to skip in big circles with other humans. Okay, so I'm not a grown-up yet. So what? I got to be a very tall ten-year-old for three days and two nights. Maybe I'll make a movie out of it.

Surfing with Insanity

❧ My wheel bearings are coming loose, the ones controlling my sanity. Domestic demands are squeezing out my writing time and the veins on my neck are standing up in protest.

Wolfe does not understand the words, "Get your shoes on." He doesn't realize that his feet have to be covered before we can leave for school. Who does he think he is, a hobbit? Finally after six or eight reminders it begins to dawn on him that today is a school day.

Talk about hyperactive, the watchword of the '90s—I'm ready to propel myself into orbit just to avoid getting him ready for school in the morning.

In the kitchen, Michael is calmly eating toast while my neck bulges and my blood boils reciting the four-year-old program of brush your teeth and hair, put on your socks and shoes. I've given up on the hair. I figure cavities are more expensive than what people will think seeing his rag-top head.

As my father used to say, "I'm headed for an early grave." Now I know what he meant. But that's a cop-out to up and die. Then who would yell at the kid to get going?

My neck muscles are so cinched I can't even talk normally. Threats zing through the air like razor blades flying past the ears.

When the therapist suggested he was hyperactive, at first I denied it. Then, I paused and felt that finally someone, a trained professional even, knows what I'm going through. I get no sympathy from stay-at-home moms trailing placid little girls who never zigzag through trash cans while standing on the seat of their bikes.

If I could just remember that doing my writing is a massage in itself. After four years of writing everyday, wouldn't that truth sink in?

Oh God. I feel so hemmed in and cloistered. I want to get out more and quit this beaten-to-a-pulp attitude.

I'm typing up poems to submit for a contest and the printer gets funky on me. I called Michael three times at work just to find out how to change the font spacing on the screen and I kept thinking, I'm an artist. I don't understand machines that hum loudly and ask questions.

Cheesh.

Almost to the breaking and snarling point, I retreated to my notebook to write and silently proclaimed that I wasn't going to the Cub Scout Olympics tonight, and prayed for Michael's return so he could take him. I needed a break so my blood vessels wouldn't burst.

Oh sure, Michael gets the accolades while I stay home, earning money, doing the laundry, getting the gas, taking Wolfe to Blockbuster to accost innocent prospective buyers of Cub Scout candy bars and even sinking so low as to clean our bathroom with bleach, no less. Even I couldn't stand it anymore.

I thought when Michael got a job I'd have more time to write, paint, film and spread my creative wings. But now I find I don't have time to cut my toenails or clear my throat.

He gets the new job as a ceramicist and talks glowingly about his love for clay, while I grouse in the background about being buried alive under an avalanche of domestic servitude and the pressure of running "our" photography business myself. Where, in this equation, is the time "to be a writer"?

Well, I've had it. I can't keep up with the laundry and vacuuming and trying behavior modification on Wolfe for "hyperactivity." It ain't flying. Plus, meet with all our clients, do the reprint orders, solicit new business and somehow stay on top of proofing. I could use ten hours more a day just to do what I'm doing now.

I have to quit doing so much. Why do I have to be everyone's answered prayer?

Not anymore.

I need to get to a garden, an ocean, a forest once a week. This will divert me from being a serial mom. Wolfe calls me "scary Mama" when I lose it over his depleted holey sock supply that he tosses into the air dirty and rolled up, never to touch hot water again, turning into large dust balls hidden in various locations around the house. Then, when he does have his socks on, he's out walking the dog (after constant begging, threats and yells) around the block. He doesn't understand that socks are meant to be worn on feet that are inside shoes and not padding along on concrete for miles.

I told him to get his jim jams on about twelve times last night, in between my cleaning the kitchen and advising Michael on contract negotiation with a bride and groom who now all of a sudden want us to videotape their wedding, but don't want to pay extra.

Michael gave me a reprieve for the Cub Scout Olympics, but I went anyway when Wolfe said, "Don't you want to see me win?" Who can resist that sweet face above a Cub Scout shirt that's too big for him? Of course I went.

All heated up without the promise of a cold
glass of wine or a double, I showed up at the
Olympics just in time to get a chance at chipping
away my rock-hard facade. Seeing the kids' eager
faces in Cub Scout caps started to melt my resolve
to be pissed off.

The scoutmaster's hairy legs in shorts, barking
the announcements through a megaphone, made
me wish I hadn't eaten all that cheese before rushing out the door to get here. I didn't want to throw
up during the three-legged race.

Wolfe was lit up. He's been holed up with
"scary Mama" every day, "doing" homework, playing on the Internet and professionally pestering
me by demanding to know where a blank cassette
is, while I'm on the phone talking money, and
insisting I look at the spot where his goldfish
landed on the floor after it jumped out of the bowl,
when I'm explaining to him that school started five
minutes ago.

I forgot about all that when Wolfe and I were
called up to be in the orange relay race. I didn't
know what it meant either. You just neck with the
person in front of you while trying to grab on to
the orange under their chin. No problem for a
Syracuse gal. I just rooted under Jack's chin and
grabbed the orange out after burrowing the upper

part of my torso around his throat. It was easy for an in-your-face New Yorker to do. But Jack is only nine so he didn't want to make out with a forty-year-old woman. I passed the orange to Wolfe, who slightly resisted my nuzzling, but clomped on to the fruit at the last second and successfully gave it to Jared behind him. One drop and we'd have to start all over again!

We won! By whole minutes, way out in front ahead of all the other teams!

A mother shouted to me, "Have you been practicing that at home?"

I haven't done that in thirty years!

I was ecstatic. I felt extaordinarily gifted to be able to pass an orange under my chin to another human being without dropping it. It was like winning the gold medal and just moments before I hadn't known what an orange relay race was. Leave it to the Cub Scouts to teach me something new. I waved my arms above my head in victory, yelled and stamped my feet and watched with pity as the other five teams struggled with their oranges, straggling minutes behind us. We won!

I was now officially out of my funk. I decided a dose of enthusiasm can cure anything and it certainly doesn't hurt to win first place in a competition in which the rest of the participants are squirming like earthworms, desperately trying to catch up to the winners—us!

And I thought I didn't want to go.

A Boy Scout Olympics is the definition of good clean fun. I could think about washing dishes later. This is what life is really about. Being able to pass an orange to another person using only your neck and chin, hands clasped behind your back. It was an accomplishment that I'll remind myself of when the chips are down and scattered around my ankles.

You just never know where you're going to get cheered up next or how a smile can return to your face when the tidal wave of life knocks you over and you don't have a surfboard.

Hey, after winning that orange relay maybe I'll even try surfing.

Wolfe the Guru

ᘒ Ten years ago today I was in labor, about to have a baby.

Back then I had no idea what it would be like to live with a preteen. Now I am contemplating where to string the crepe-paper tails and I realize that the ice-cream cake needs picking up, his big present needs wrapping and we need one more treat bag because Wolfe fell in love with a new friend yesterday and he had to be invited.

I am going to allow seven ten-year-old boys to sleep in my basement tonight. They won't actually fall asleep until 2 or 3 AM and will have to be threatened within an inch of their lives that their parents will be called if they don't fall asleep NOW. We did this last year so I know what to expect. Wolfe came upstairs and slept in his own bed at about 2:30AM because Teddy kept farting on his head. And still I go forward and allow my brain to be fried for hours, just to let the little skippers have a thrilling ride into the wee hours of the morning.

I'm sure it's something that could be cleared up with a little psychotherapy.

It's been a whole decade! Ten years ago I was leaking lochia from every pore and now I'm his limo driver, escorting him to play practice and the bead shop to buy more baubles. He insists that I should let him ride his bike downtown alone. "Brian rides his bike to school alone!" I can't let him do that until he's at least thirty. We are only ten blocks from his school, but there are heavily trafficked streets in between that have come close to running me down when I thought I was paying attention. I am not going to trust my only begotten son to the scattered minds of half-asleep commuters frantic to get to work, waking up behind the wheel of a car, coffee cups glued to their faces. My kid is not coming home in a body bag. Wolfe has heard that so many times that he repeats it along with me as I say it. What am I going to do when he wants to go out with girls? Drive them around and make sure they don't make out, which can and does lead to premarital sex?

Okay, tomorrow he turns ten and I'm going to celebrate that. When I first laid eyes on him ten years ago I had no idea what I was in for. He can charm the yesses right out of me, get free candy from 7-11 cashiers, choose the best table in a restaurant and figure out a great birthday gift for me. He knows his own mind, sports purple hair,

rides his bike like a professional stunt driver and
stands on the seat when I tell him NO. Even crash-
ing into that concrete wall didn't stop him. Now he
has a "cool scar" on his lip and he dreams of
getting an even more expensive trick bike, presumably to perform aerial stunts before a crowd. And
people ask me, "You just have the one?" Yes, and
my heart is lodged in my throat daily, just considering what he'll do next. That's why I decided to
make a film out of it. So I could laugh at myself
and provide entertainment at the same time.

Now that he's in the preteen years I am just
now realizing that teenhood and cars and exposure
to drugs comes next. I hope he's a lot smarter
than his mother was. I cringe remembering what I
was doing as a teenager, and even he recoils when
I tell him I smoked pot, as if I just revealed that I
was a crack addict. I'm sure he'll turn out much
better than I did. For one thing, he swears less
than I do. And he's even starting to comb his hair
and apply creme rinse spray to keep it in place. He
thinks cigarettes are stupid and that cancer is way
uncool. He wants a woman for the presidency next
and insists that I vote for her. He made me feel
ashamed that I voted for Clinton last time. The
least I could have done was vote for Ralph Nader.
The upshot is I have more to learn from him than

he does from me. There, I've said it again. There's
no ego in that; it is just the truth. And that's what
my short film is about: Wolfe has more to teach us
than we have to teach him. Yes, I know we keep
him safe and steer him towards his own personal
victories, but he's the one that smacks me in the
face with a cornstalk and delivers some searing bit
of truth that I hadn't thought of.

The truth is so inconvenient.

He's also nicer than me, at least to other people
who do not have the power to tell him when he
has to go to bed. In short, he is my live-in shooting
star, my mind-opening tornado on wheels who
obliterates my carefully concealed attempts at
staying small. Being ten is no picnic when you
have to teach your parents so much. That's okay. I
stand stubbornly waiting for my next volley of
scorn, when it is again revealed that I am way
behind the program.

I really unhinged his shaky belief in my sanity
when we were watching TV last night and I admit-
ted that I just now realized we were looking at the
Star Trek TV trailers and not the film version. His
eyes said it all. It really keeps the spice in our
mother-child bond when I can be totally naked of all
ego and just let him point out my inadequacies with
his amusing and shaken-to-the-core sense of reality.

And you thought having kids would be easy. It isn't. It's a constant reminder that I'm slipping behind.

Fine. Let him go ahead. I'll give him the keys to my car and he can drive me around.

৯৶ Thank you for buying this book.

Now my kid can go to college.

I can be reached at www.mary@nanospace.com

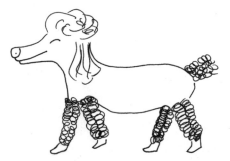